Top Speed Team-Ups

Written & Illustrated by
Gregg Schigiel

HATTER
entertainment

Editor: Polly Watson
Cover illustration and design: Gregg Schigiel
Book design: Gregg Schigiel

Thanks: Tom Brevoort, Jerzy Drozd, Chris
Giarrusso, Mark Waid and Mike Wieringo

ZOOPERHERO UNIVERSE: TOP SPEED TEAM-UPS. Published by Hatter Entertainment, hatterentertainment.com.
Copyright © 2022 Gregg Schigiel. All rights reserved. "ZOOPERHERO UNIVERSE," its logos, and the likenesses of all characters
herein are trademarks of Gregg Schigiel, unless otherwise noted. "Hatter Entertainment" and the Hatter Entertainment
logos are trademarks of Hatter Entertainment. No part of this publication may be reproduced or transmitted, in any form
or by any means (except for short excerpts for journalistic or review purposes), without the express written permission of
Gregg Schigiel. All names, characters, events, and locales in this publication are entirely fictional. Any resemblance to actual
persons (living or dead), events, or places, without satiric intent, is coincidental.

ISBN: 978-0-9905218-6-0

TABLE OF CONTENTS

CHAPTER ONE

Questions and Answers

"…and that's what it's like for me being the world's fastest zooperhero," said Quickfast, finishing her presentation to the third and fourth graders at Sigma City Elementary School. They were seated on the floor with their full attention on the hero in front of them. "Does anyone have any questions?"

Almost every paw and claw and hoof and wing shot into the air. There were a lot of questions.

Ms. Perry, the school librarian, stood up and walked to where Quickfast stood and asked quietly, "Do you have time for this?"

"Oh, I'll make it *quick*," Quickfast said, clicking her tongue twice to accentuate her pun. And with that, she started taking questions from the class.

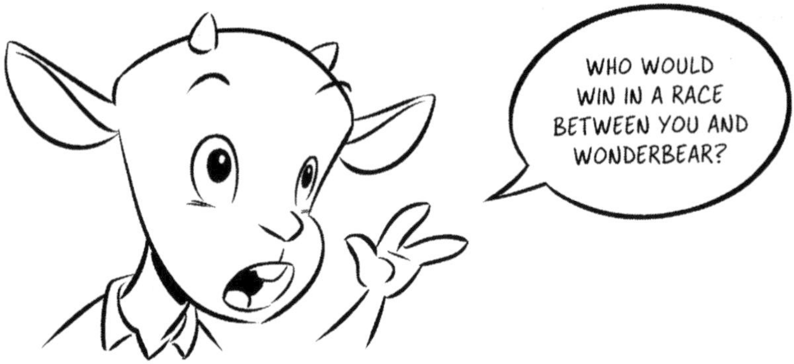
WHO WOULD WIN IN A RACE BETWEEN YOU AND WONDERBEAR?

"Well, the times I've been around him and we were on the move, he was flying and I was on the ground, so we've never had a proper one-on-one running race. But, as fast as he is…if we were both on foot, I mean, come on, I'm Quickfast over here!" she answered confidently.

A young beaver asked, "Who is your most worstest nemesis?"

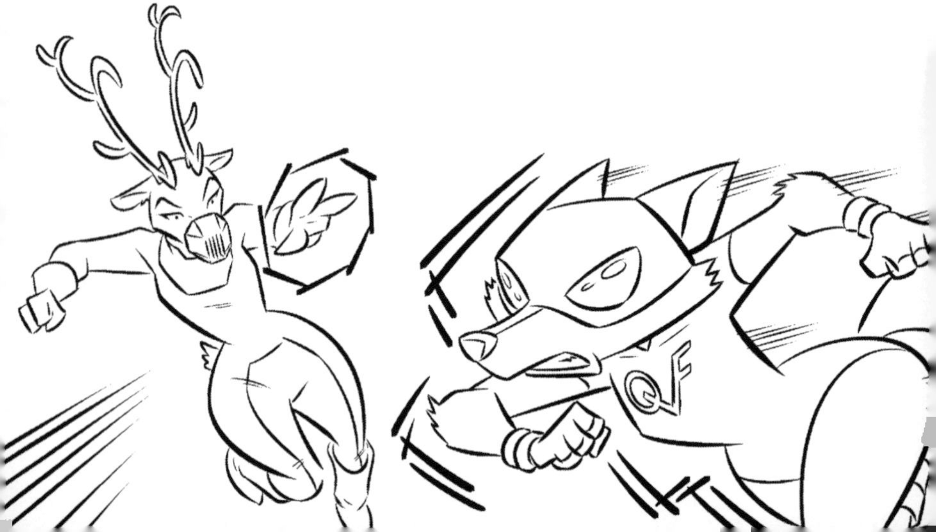

"Probably Red Light," answered Quickfast. "Because she can stop things in their tracks, I can't rely as much on moving fast. I have to think fast."

WOULD YOU EVER JOIN THE JUSTICE BRIGADE?

"Hm, good question. They haven't asked me...yet. But honestly, I can be in like, three or four places at once, so I'm kinda like my own Justice Brigade," she answered, totally self-assured.

"Have you ever met Flexi-Bill?" asked a young goose.

"I have, he's funny," replied Quickfast.

"Have you ever met Barbearian?" asked a quiet armadillo.

"Briefly. She's intense, but cool," offered Quickfast.

"Have you ever met Hop Chop and Shellshot?" asked an excitable bunny.

"Yes. They're rad. Very competitive," answered Quickfast.

"Have you ever met Ahdduk the Mystic?" asked an anxious rhinoceros.

"Him I have not met," replied Quickfast, "But I've heard he's not as creepy strange as he appears?"

A young deer started to ask, "Have you ever met—" when Ms. Perry interrupted them before they could finish their question.

"Children, let's ask Quickfast questions about her, not about who she has or hasn't met, okay?"

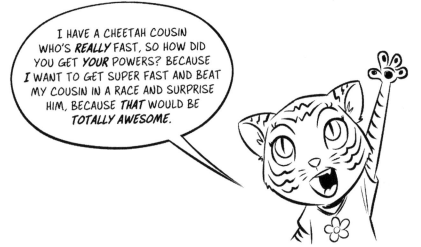

I HAVE A CHEETAH COUSIN WHO'S *REALLY* FAST, SO HOW DID YOU GET *YOUR* POWERS? BECAUSE *I* WANT TO GET SUPER FAST AND BEAT MY COUSIN IN A RACE AND SURPRISE HIM, BECAUSE *THAT* WOULD BE *TOTALLY AWESOME.*

The class laughed at the young tiger's question. But they all wanted to know the answer. After hearing Quickfast's presentation, every one of them imagined how amazing it would be to have super-speed powers.

"Y'know," answered Quickfast with a bit of a sigh, "that's the one question I can't answer. Not because I don't know how I got my powers. I totally know that. So I could tell you, but I actually can't tell you.

"The thing is, I got my powers totally by accident. It was a freak event that even if it could be re-created, shouldn't be because it could be super dangerous.

"So to be sure that doesn't happen...to make certain that none of you little critters try something foolish like try to give yourselves super-speed powers"—she clicked her tongue twice, again, as if to say, *I'm on to you kids*—"and actually get hurt or worse, I don't talk about it. Sorry, gang."

The children all rumbled and mumbled.

"But instead of that, for my last thing, how about everyone make a paper airplane and throw it at me. I'll catch all of them before they hit the ground."

All the children cheered and got to work on their paper airplanes.

Quickfast smiled at Ms. Perry. Ms. Perry politely smiled back, but the truth was she didn't love that Quickfast was riling the kids up and then leaving her to handle them.

Once all the planes were made, they threw them toward Quickfast.

And of course Quickfast caught them all; moreover, she autographed each one for the kids to have as a souvenir.

The kids applauded and hooted and hollered with glee. And in a flash, Quickfast was gone.

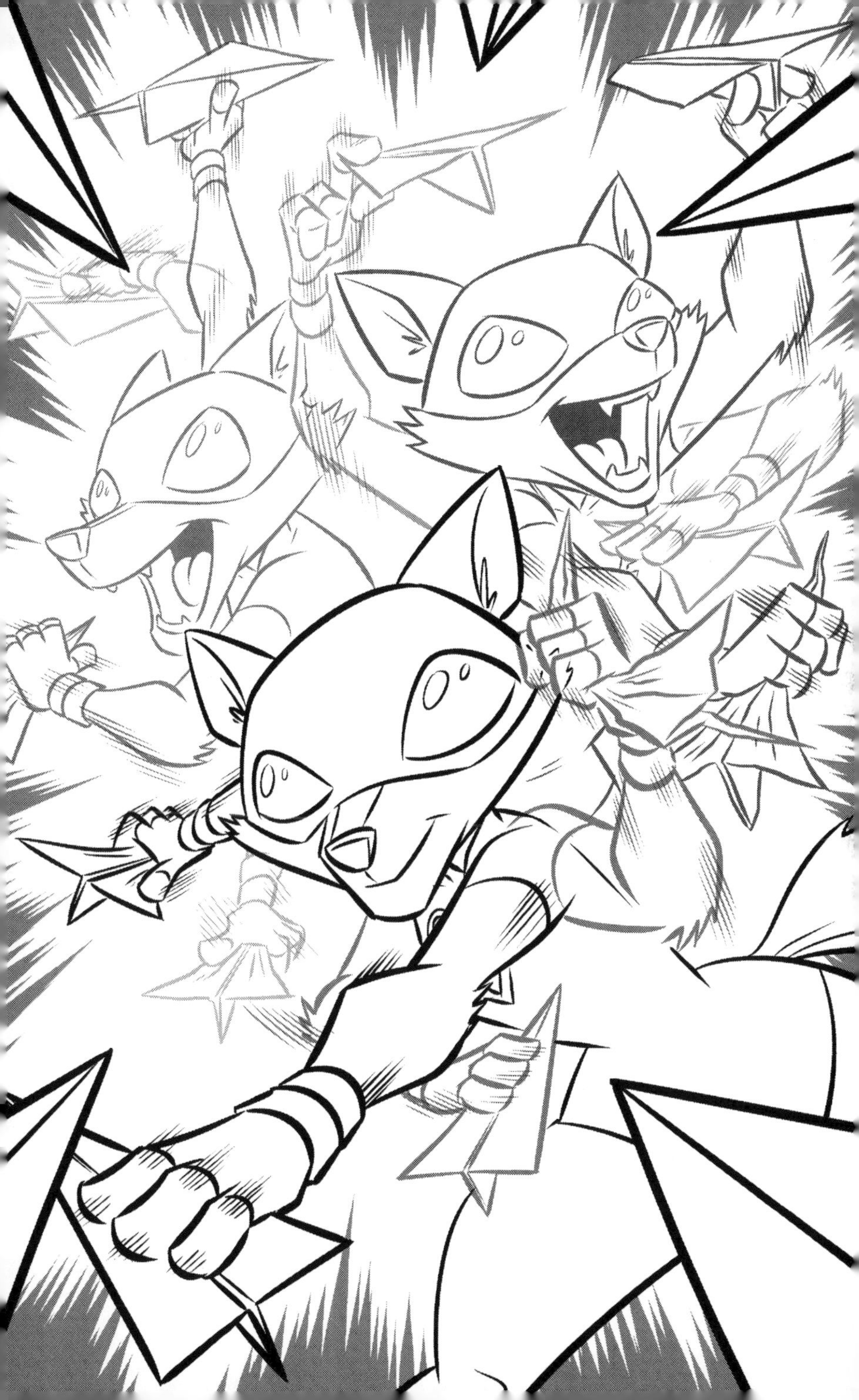

As Quickfast ran from the school to her next destination, she was pretty pleased with herself. She usually was. Quickfast had a lot of self-confidence and pretty much was convinced she could handle anything. In fact, she'd probably want to narrate this book. And if she did, she'd likely start by saying…

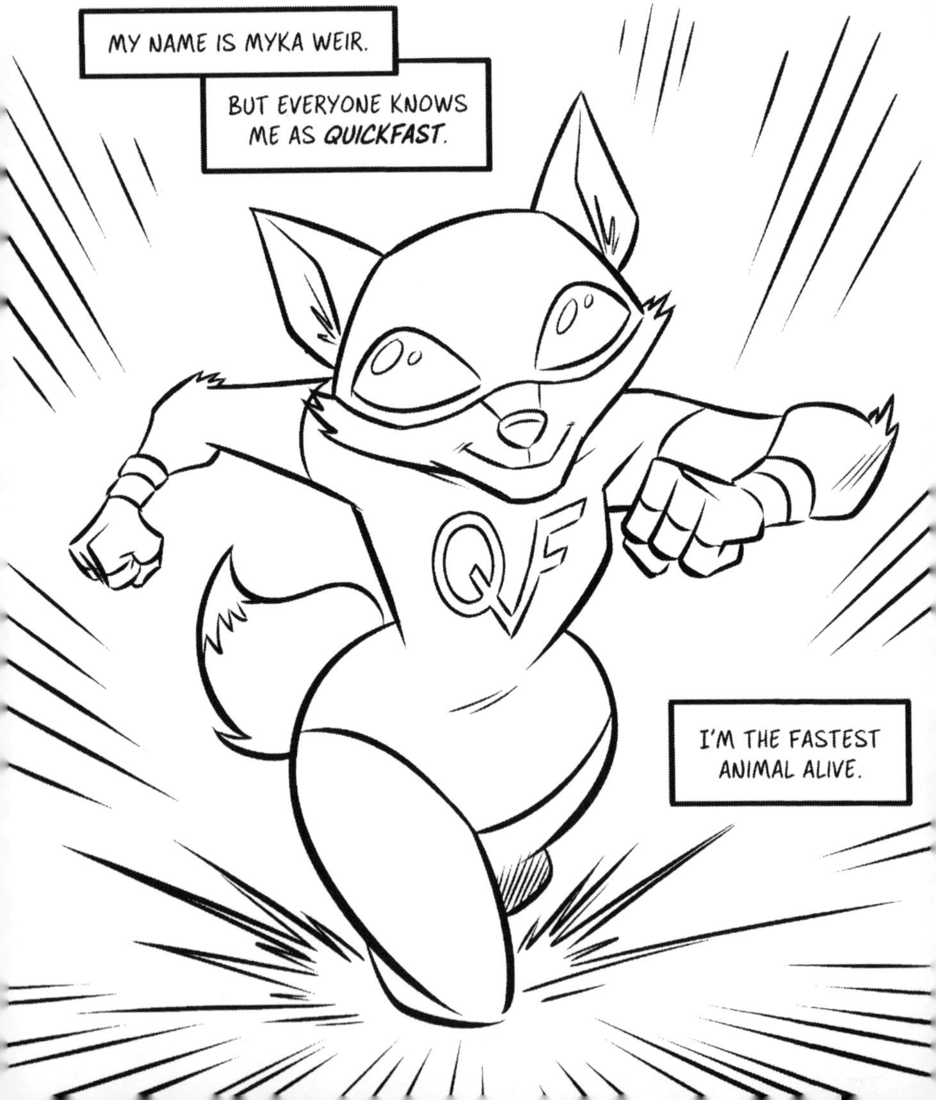

MY NAME IS MYKA WEIR.
BUT EVERYONE KNOWS ME AS *QUICKFAST*.
I'M THE FASTEST ANIMAL ALIVE.

CHAPTER TWO

Ice and Water

Quickfast was making her way from Sigma City toward Delta City. It was just over 600 miles. And while most animals would take a plane or train or drive, Quickfast was faster than any car, train, or airplane, so she was running it. It wouldn't take too long, really. Though she would need to make stops along the way to eat.

What she didn't expect was bad weather. Every forecast she'd read mentioned clear skies and mild temperatures. She was looking forward to that. She even decided to run up the coast to take in the view of the ocean. But about fifty miles outside of Sigma City, as she approached a coastal port town, something strange happened.

It was springtime, and she was far enough south that it shouldn't have been cold out. But Quickfast felt a chill and could see her own breath. This was very, very odd.

She ran quickly up and down the streets of the town and there, at the pier, she saw what was happening: Watermane, the aquatic Zooperhero, was locked in battle with an ice-powered sheep named Coldfront.

From what Quickfast could see, Coldfront had the upper hand, as the frigid foe was easily using Watermane's water-based powers against him.

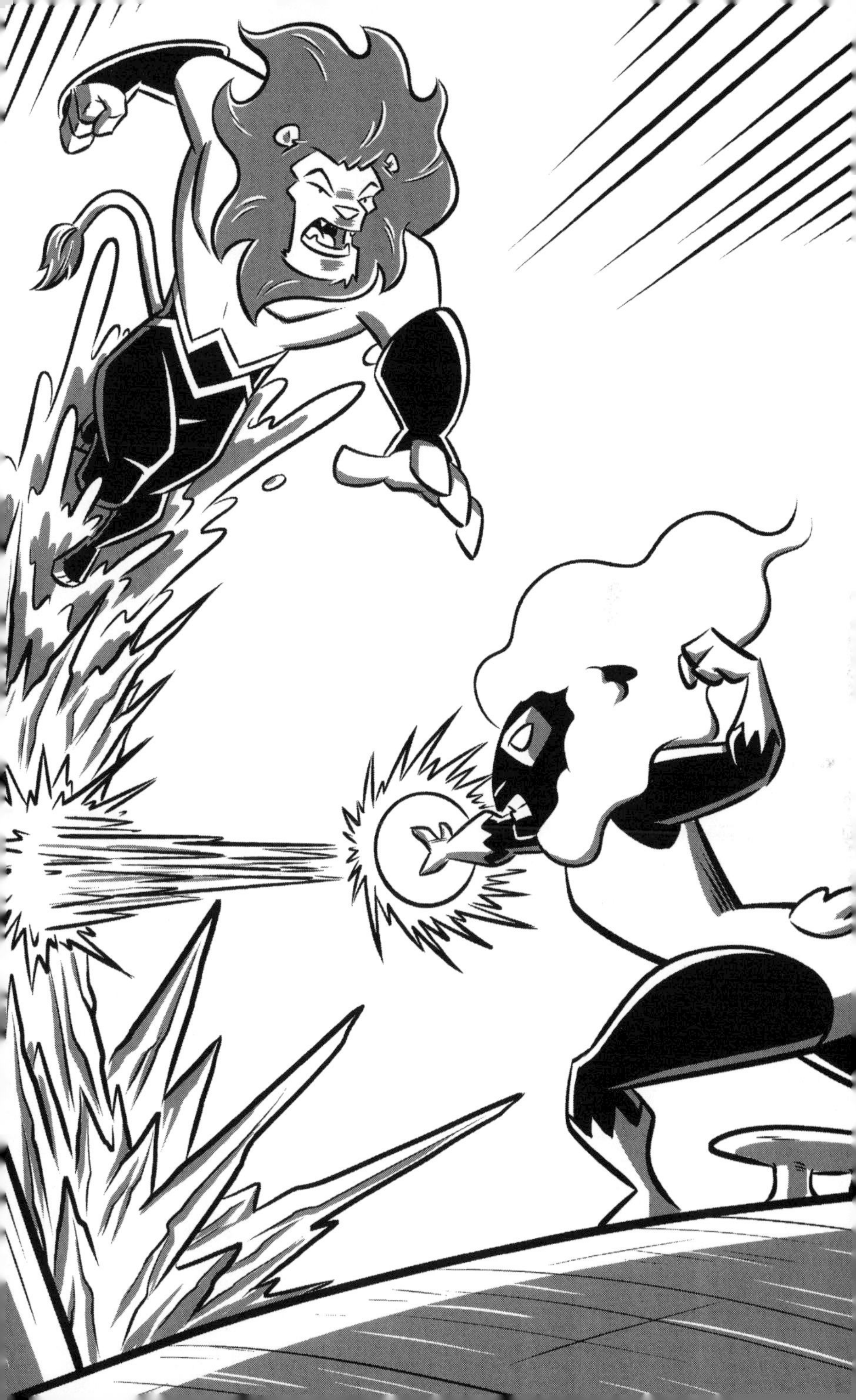

"Hey, Watermane," called out Quickfast, "looks like you could use a hand."

"Quickfast!" Watermane exclaimed, turning to see the fleet fox. "You're right about that. Coldfront's frozen me in my own water propulsion stream!"

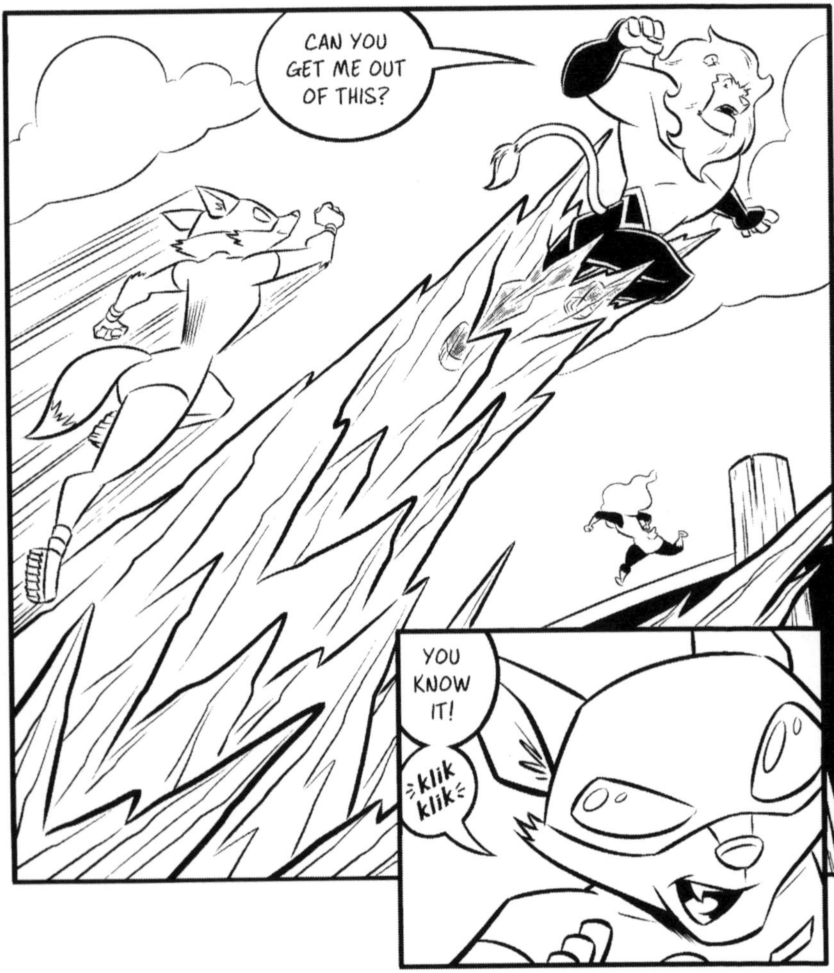
CAN YOU GET ME OUT OF THIS?
YOU KNOW IT!
klik klik

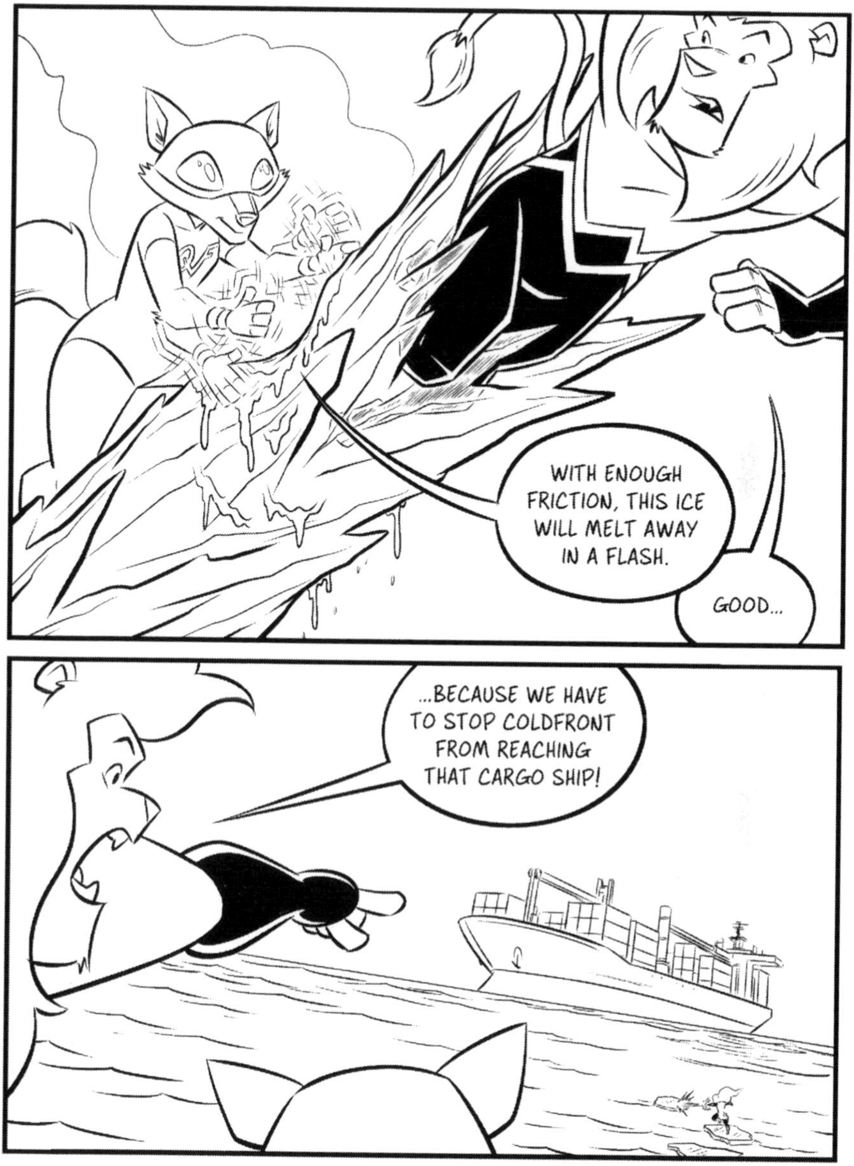
WITH ENOUGH FRICTION, THIS ICE WILL MELT AWAY IN A FLASH.
GOOD...
...BECAUSE WE HAVE TO STOP COLDFRONT FROM REACHING THAT CARGO SHIP!

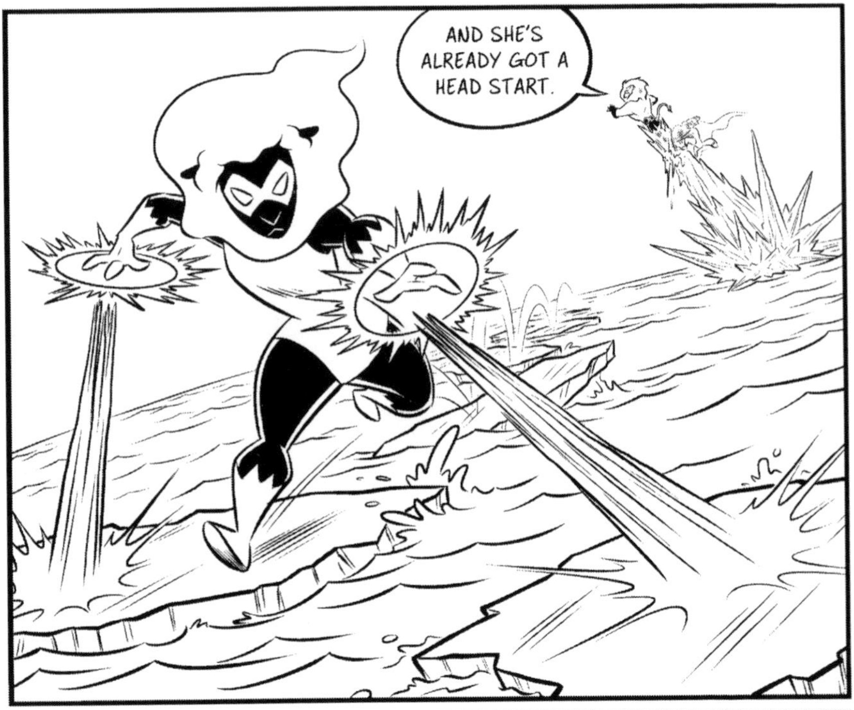
AND SHE'S ALREADY GOT A HEAD START.

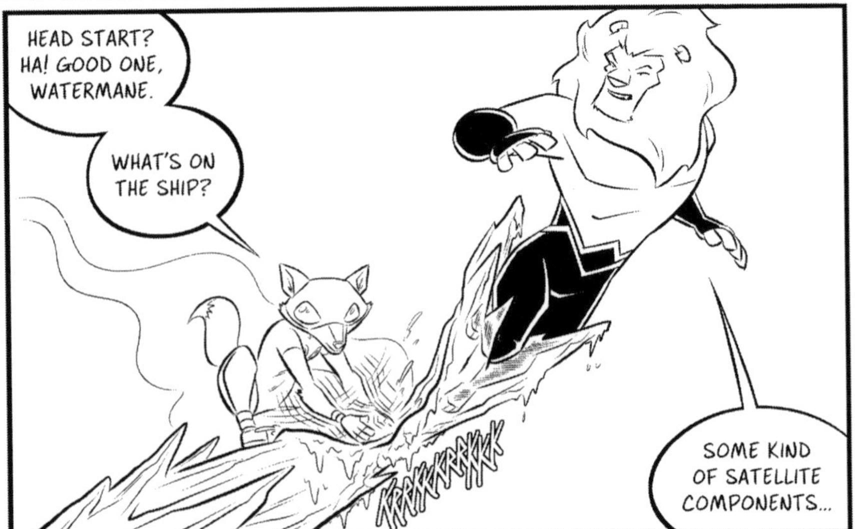
HEAD START? HA! GOOD ONE, WATERMANE.
WHAT'S ON THE SHIP?
KRRKKKRRKKK
SOME KIND OF SATELLITE COMPONENTS...

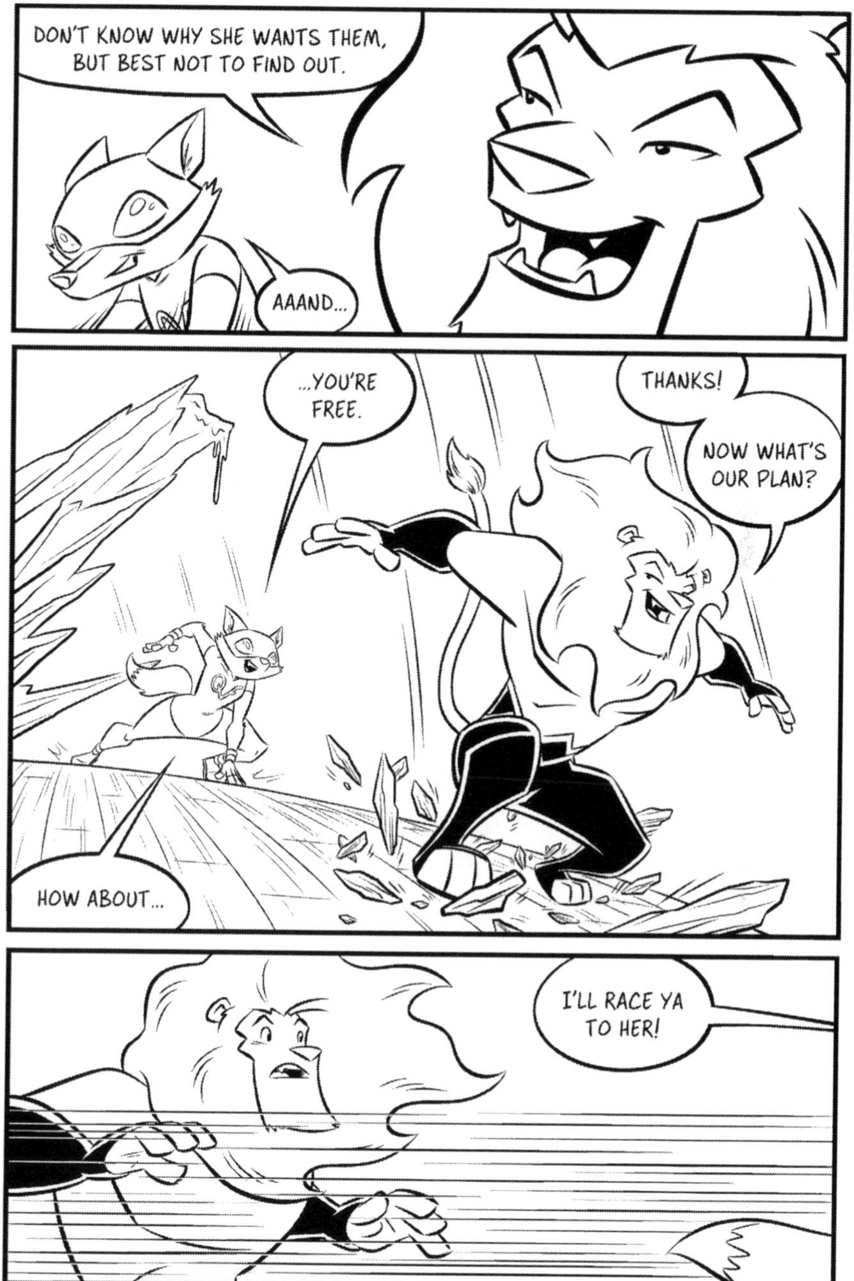
DON'T KNOW WHY SHE WANTS THEM, BUT BEST NOT TO FIND OUT.
AAAND...
...YOU'RE FREE.
THANKS!
NOW WHAT'S OUR PLAN?
HOW ABOUT...
I'LL RACE YA TO HER!

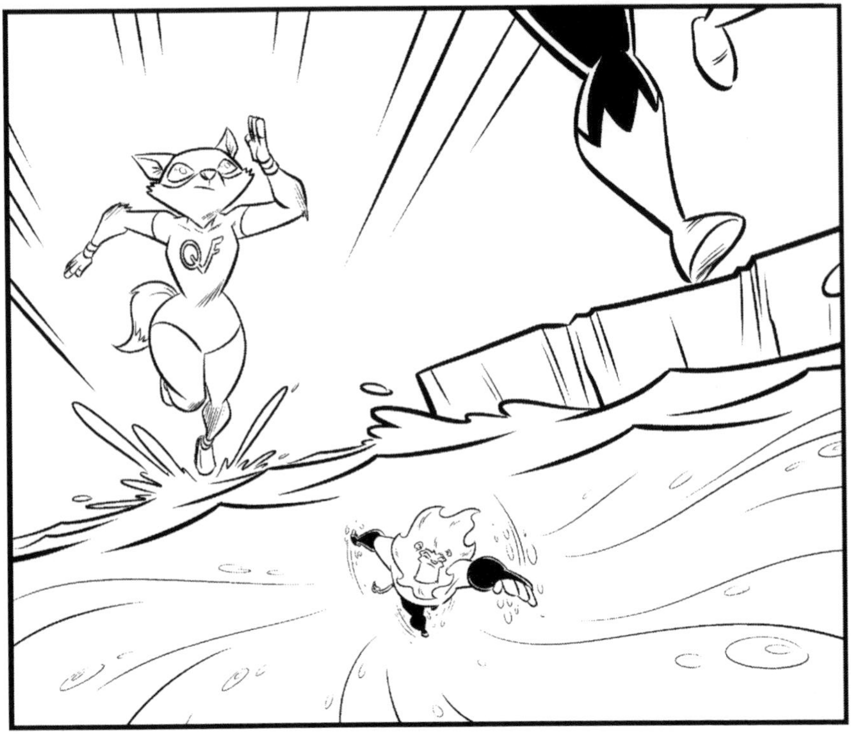

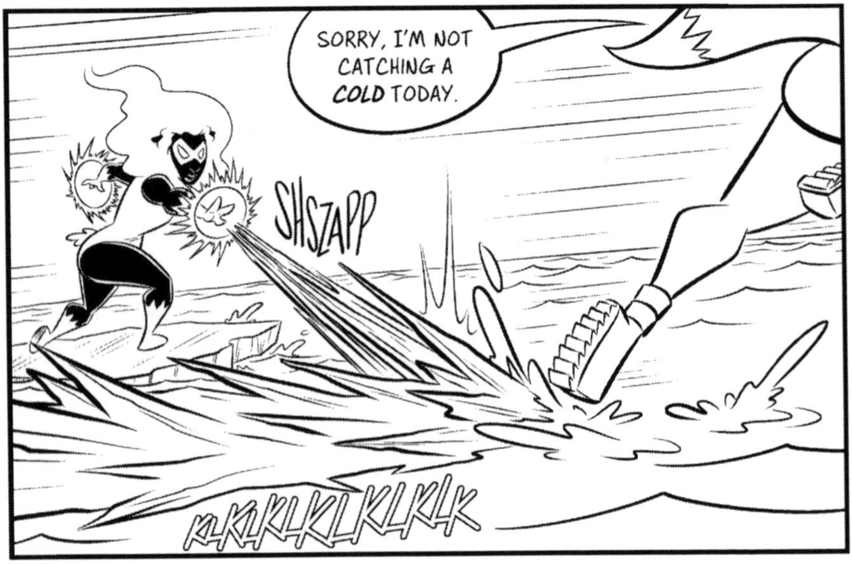
SORRY, I'M NOT CATCHING A COLD TODAY.
SHSZAPP
KLKLKLKLKLKLKLK

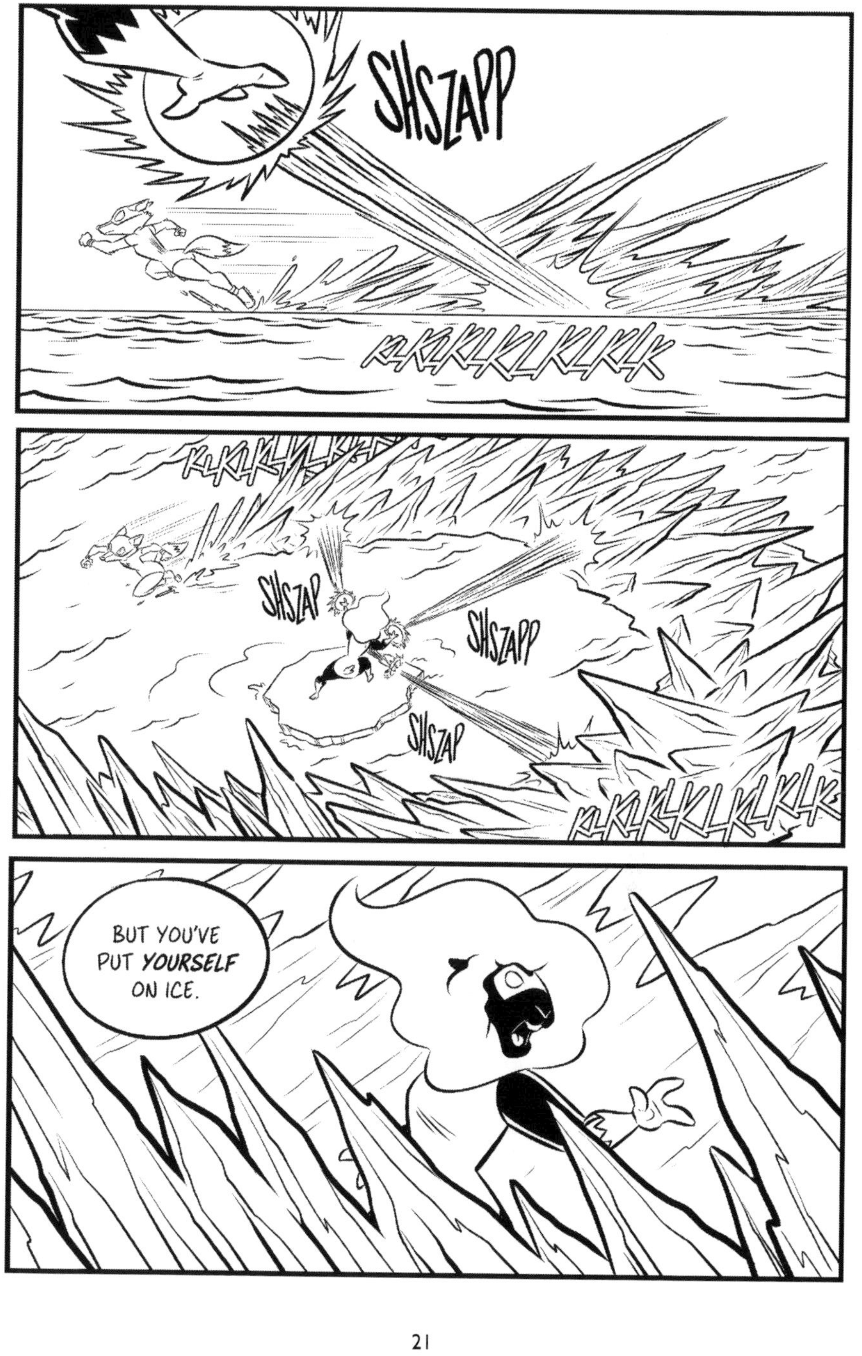
SHSZAPP
SHSZAP
SHSZAPP
SHSZAP
BUT YOU'VE PUT *YOURSELF* ON ICE.

With Coldfront trapped in an ice prison of her own making, Quickfast and Watermane regroup.

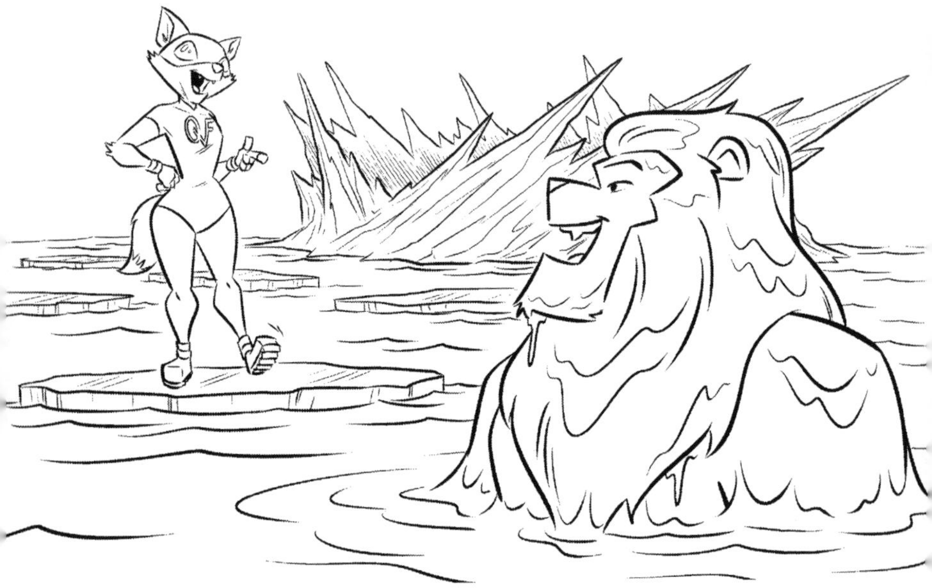
QF

“Guess I beat ya, huh, Watermane? You missed all the action,” gloated Quickfast.

“Oh, I was busy underwater, Quickfast, pulling the tide under Coldfront, sending your water trail higher,” explained Watermane. “You know what they say about only seeing the tip of the iceberg, ha ha.”

Quickfast rubbed her chin, “Hm, I guess…but I think

anyone watching would say I kinda handled this shivery sheep solo." She clicked her tongue twice.

"But hey," she added, "If you think you can handle things alone from here, I've gotta split."

Watermane looked at the defeated Coldfront. "I've got this," he said, a little annoyed at Quickfast's ego.

But she didn't catch that, as Quickfast…

…took off, continuing on her way.

CHAPTER THREE

Lightning and Bug

Quickfast had been running for about twenty minutes when something else unexpected happened. As she ran, she felt her fur start to rise off her skin. Suddenly the air around her was filled with static electricity. She slowed down.

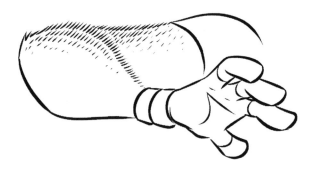

Then she smelled something in the air…a scent like burning but not burning…like an electrical wire shorting and creating a fire. Then she sensed a flash of light behind her and turned around.

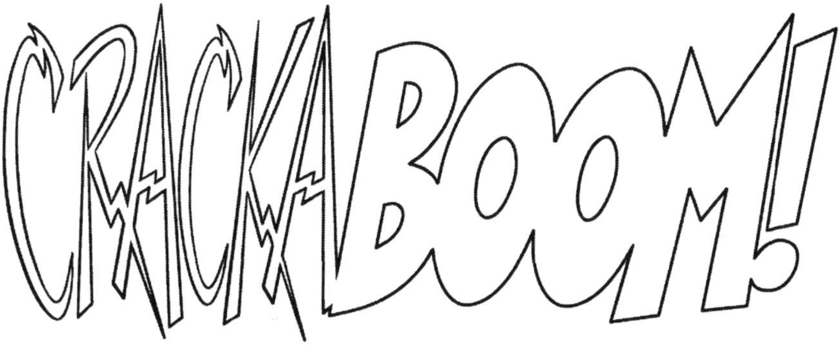
CRACKABOOM!

"Was that…thunder?" she asked herself.

And then she saw more flashing lights in the distance, behind some factory buildings. She heard more cracks and booms. She ran toward the sounds to see what was going on.

There, in the industrial part of this city, Quickfast saw another battle being waged. In this one, N-SECT, the amazing armored ant, was facing Lightning Rod, the evil, electrically charged rooster. Both hovered in the air, N-SECT firing off pulse blasts from every arm, while Lightning Rod shot bolts of lightning from his fingers. Floating behind him, in an electrical energy sphere, was a metal crate.

The bright lights and loud noise were intense. She wished in that moment that her mask covered her ears to muffle things a bit. In all that chaos, even if she wanted to call out to N-SECT that she was there to offer help, there was no way N-SECT would hear her.

But before Quickfast could say or do anything else, Lightning Rod successfully struck N-SECT with a powerful bolt of electrical energy.

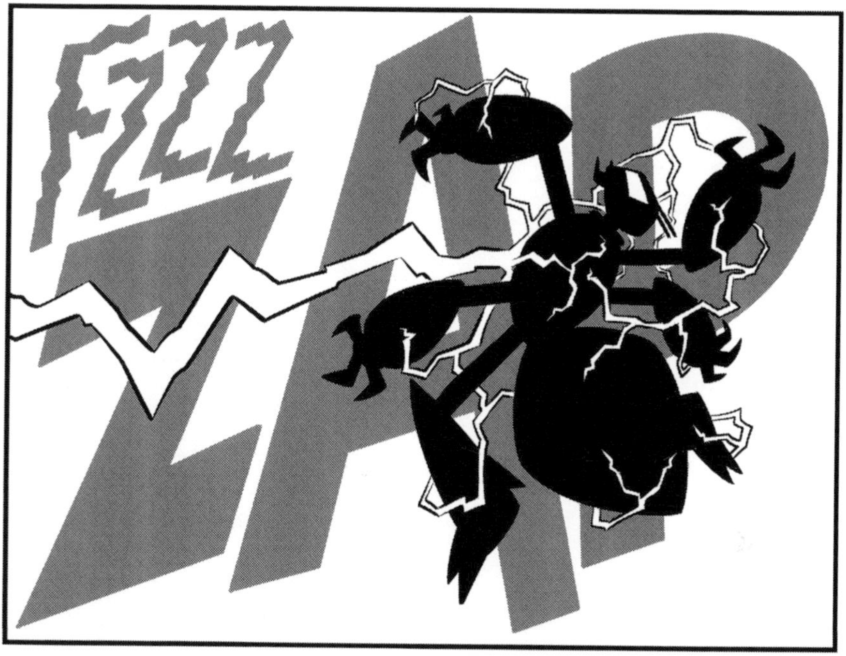

FZZZ
ZAP

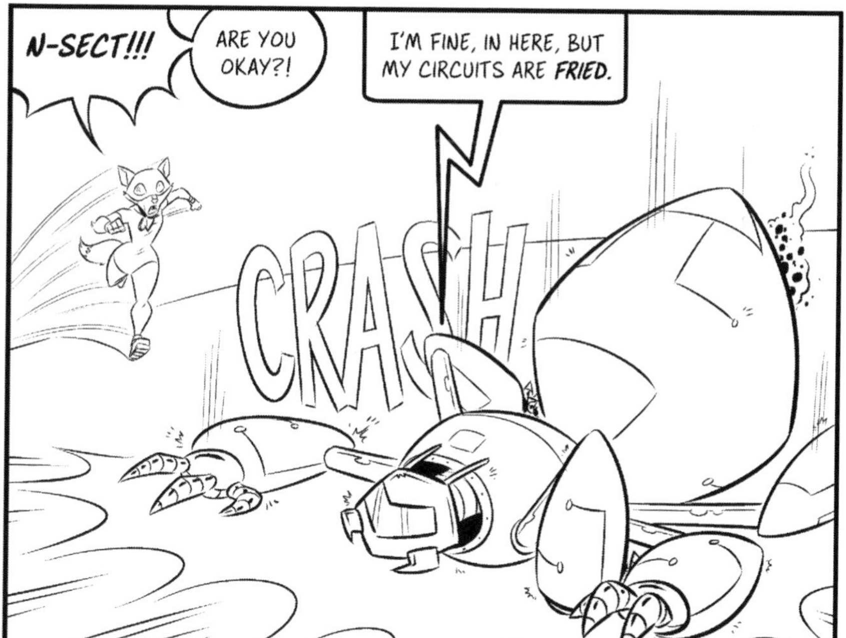

N-SECT!!!
ARE YOU OKAY?!
I'M FINE, IN HERE, BUT MY CIRCUITS ARE FRIED.
CRASH

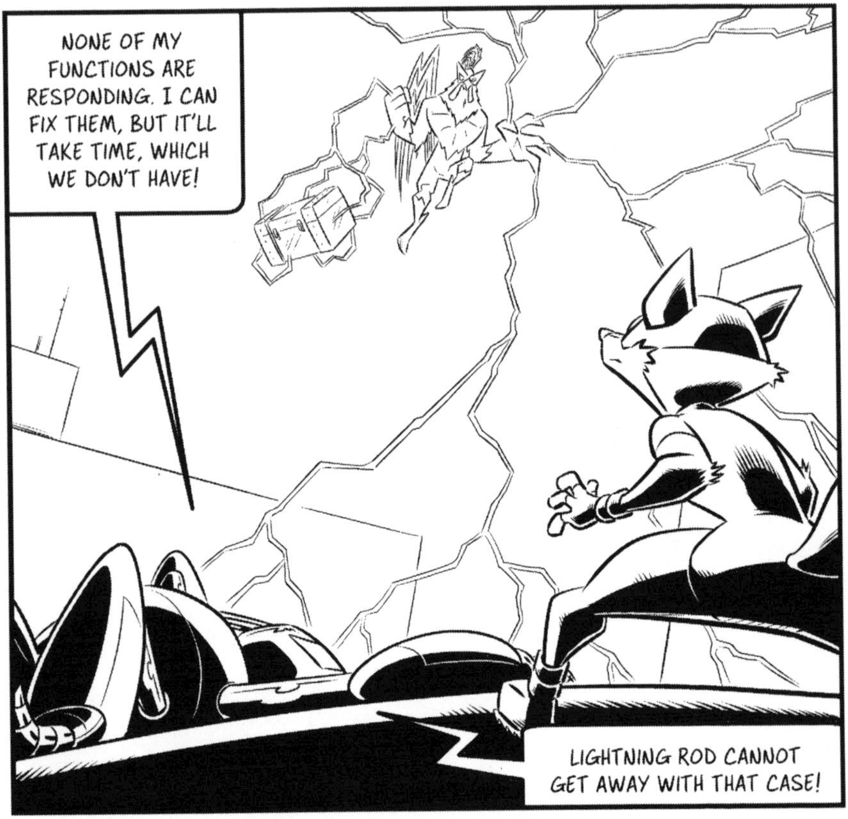
NONE OF MY FUNCTIONS ARE RESPONDING. I CAN FIX THEM, BUT IT'LL TAKE TIME, WHICH WE DON'T HAVE!
LIGHTNING ROD CANNOT GET AWAY WITH THAT CASE!

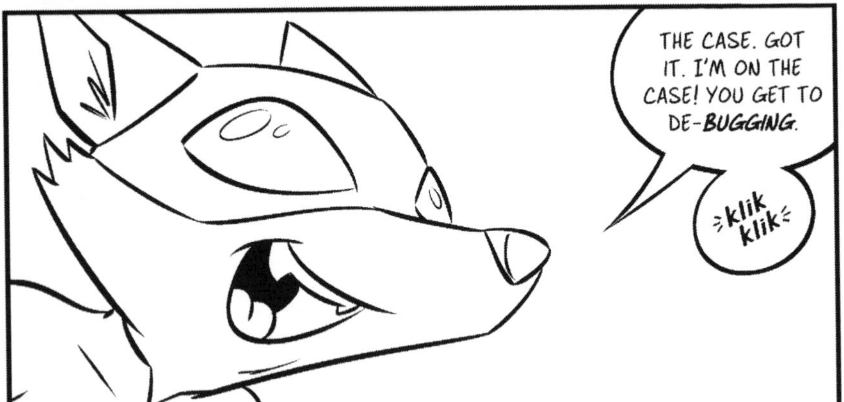
THE CASE. GOT IT. I'M ON THE CASE! YOU GET TO DE-***BUGGING***.
klik klik

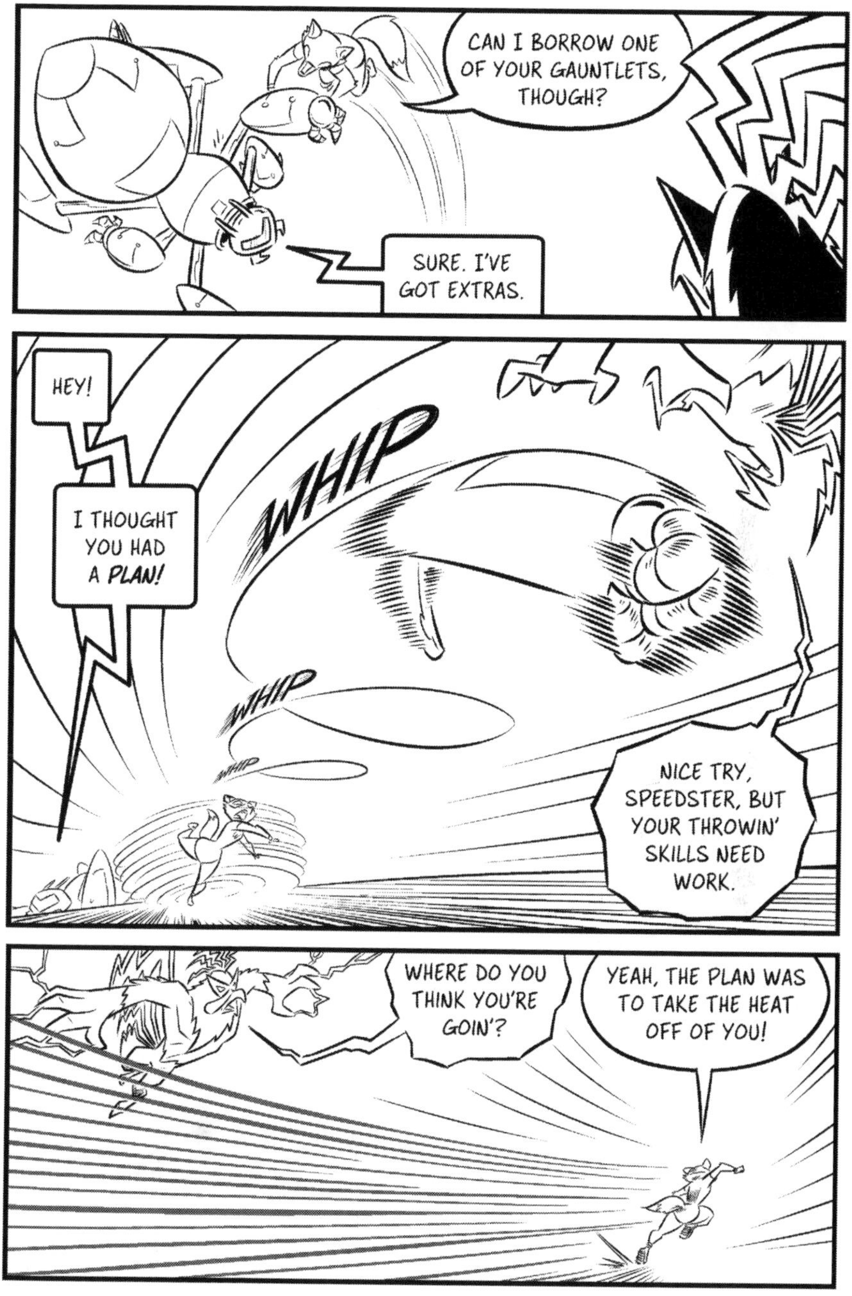
CAN I BORROW ONE OF YOUR GAUNTLETS, THOUGH?
SURE. I'VE GOT EXTRAS.
HEY!
I THOUGHT YOU HAD A *PLAN!*
WHIP
WHIP
WHIP
NICE TRY, SPEEDSTER, BUT YOUR THROWIN' SKILLS NEED WORK.
WHERE DO YOU THINK YOU'RE GOIN'?
YEAH, THE PLAN WAS TO TAKE THE HEAT OFF OF YOU!

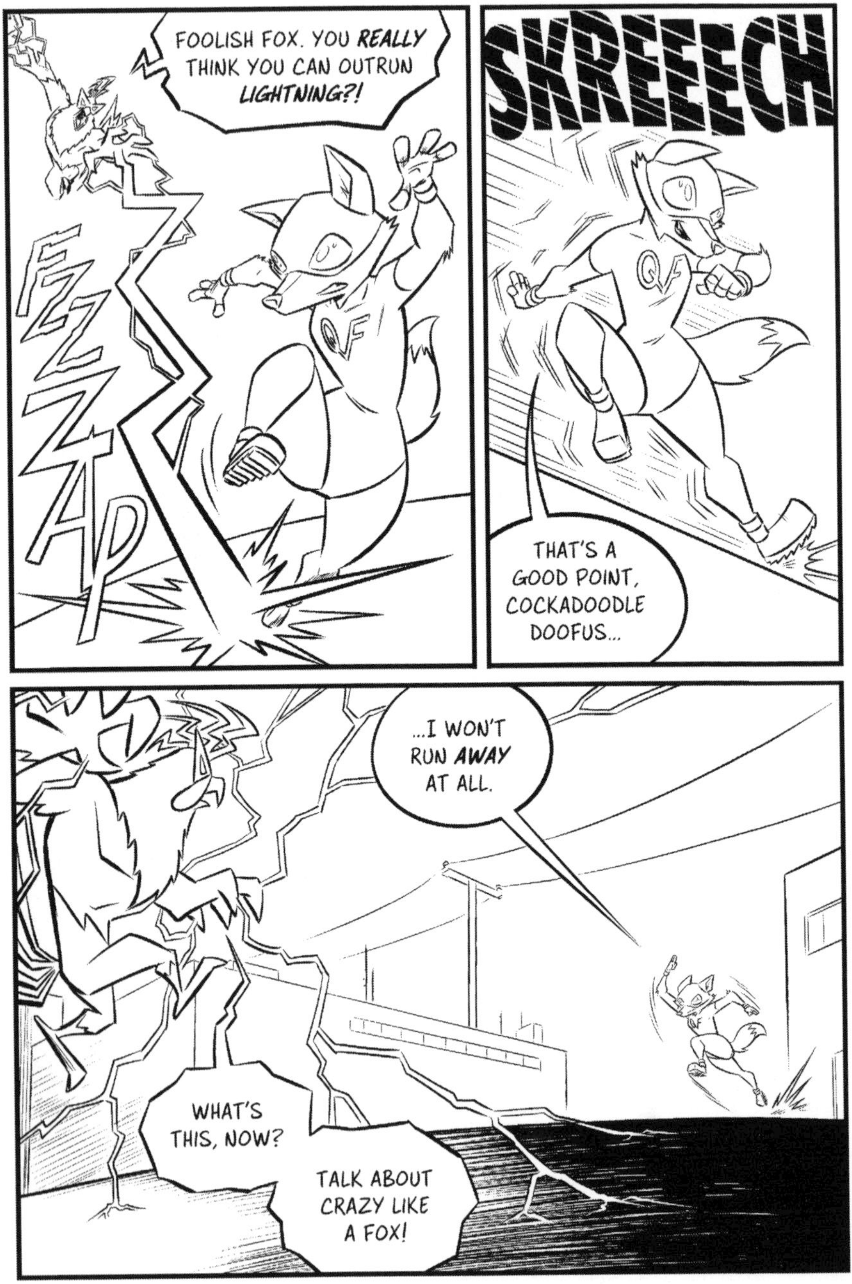
FOOLISH FOX. YOU **REALLY** THINK YOU CAN OUTRUN **LIGHTNING?!**
FZZZZAP
SKREEECH
THAT'S A GOOD POINT, COCKADOODLE DOOFUS...
...I WON'T RUN **AWAY** AT ALL.
WHAT'S THIS, NOW?
TALK ABOUT CRAZY LIKE A FOX!

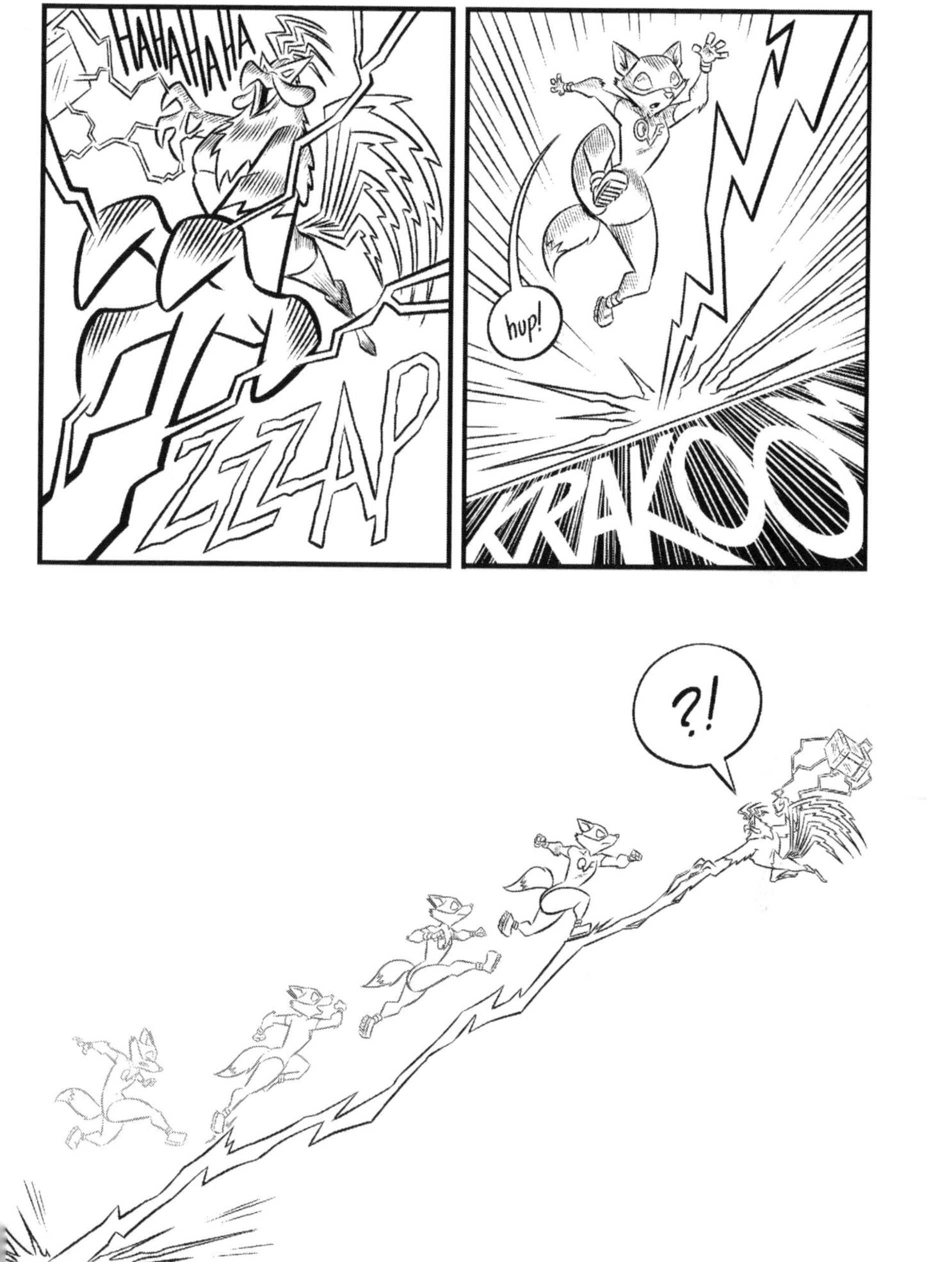
HAHAHAHA
ZZZAP
hup!
KRAKOO
?!

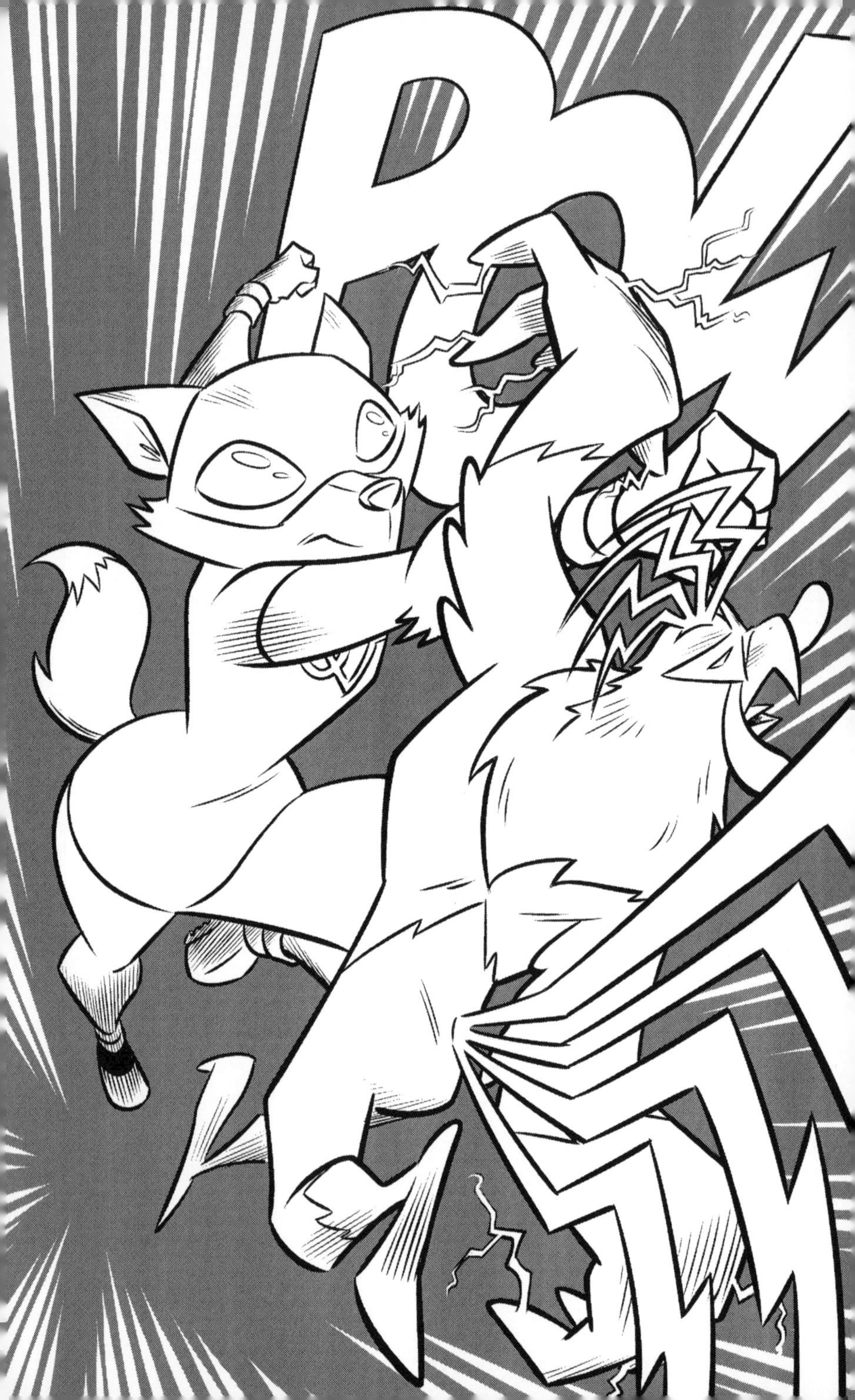

With Lightning Rod knocked out, his electrical grip on the case fizzled away. Quickfast, Lightning Rod, and the case all fell to the ground.

"I know you don't need to hear this," said N-SECT, who was back up and running, reattaching the disconnected gauntlet with one arm and grabbing the case with another, "but that was very impressive. I had no idea you could run on lightning!"

"Hey...what can I say?" responded Quickfast. She tried to brush it off. The truth was she didn't know she could run on lightning, either! But she liked that N-SECT was awed by her, and she didn't want to get in the way of or give up the compliment.

"You know," said N-SECT, "I'd really like to have you over to Justice Brigade headquarters, really put your powers to the test in my—"

"Oh, hey, listen, I appreciate the offer," interrupted Quickfast, "and I know you could probably use a speedster on your squad, but—"

N-SECT stopped her midsentence, "Oh no, I wasn't I wasn't offering a membersh—"

Quickfast then cut off N-SECT, “Well, all right, I gotta get moving. You have the case, so that’s cool. I’ll let you take care of that rascally rooster, yeah?”

And like that…

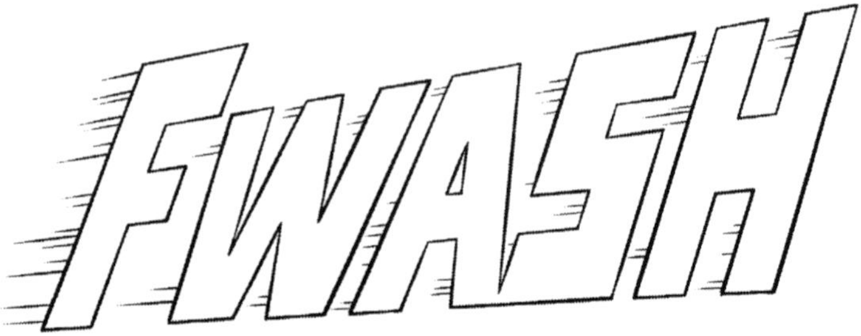
FWASH

…Quickfast was on her way, leaving N-SECT alone to deal with Lightning Rod…

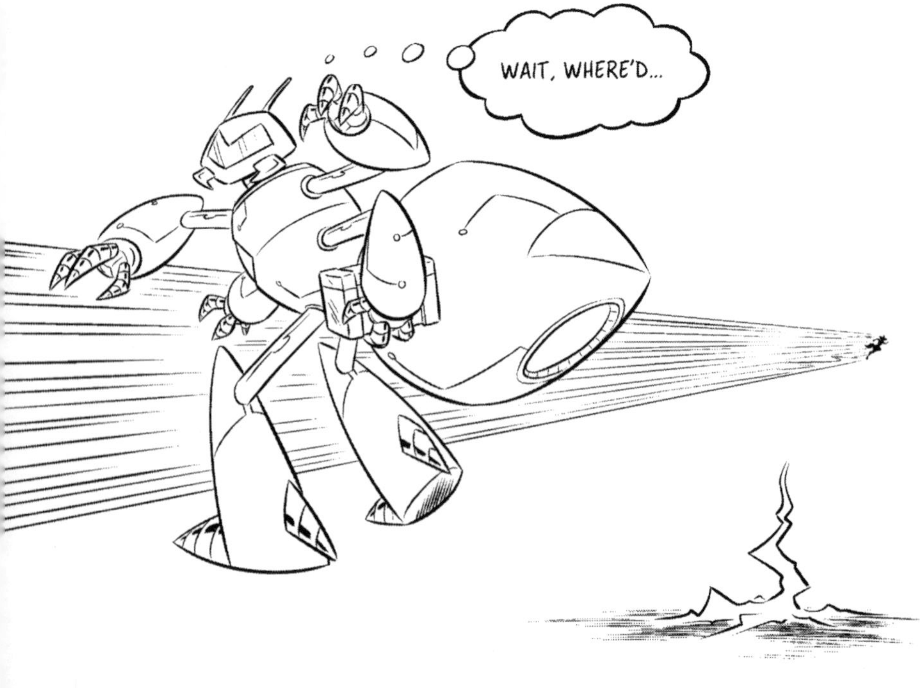
WAIT, WHERE'D...

CHAPTER FOUR

Storm and Spear

Quickfast felt especially energized after pulling off that stunt with the lightning. She was grinning widely as she ran. She'd taken a huge risk and it had paid off. She felt like she'd really leveled up as a zooperhero.

A small part of her felt bad that she hadn't admitted to N-SECT that she'd never done it before. She didn't like hiding the truth. But at the same time, there were plenty of things she wouldn't tell N-SECT. For starters, they both had secret identities!

Less of a secret was how she reacted to N-SECT mentioning the Justice Brigade. Sometimes Quickfast was moving, thinking, and reacting *too* fast and should wait until someone was finished speaking. She felt pretty embarrassed. Her ego kinda got the best of her in that moment.

Of course, all of these thoughts were really starting to rain on her parade and her excitement over what she'd done.

And speaking of rain, what should have been a beautiful day kept offering surprises. It suddenly started pouring rain thirty or forty miles outside of Gamma City. On top of that, gale force winds sent the sheets of big, heavy drops flying at a sharp angle. Quickfast had a very good suspicion by now who might be behind this storm.

Coldfront and Lightning Rod were members of a team of villains, the Barnstormers. Each member of that group had a different weather-based power. Owing to these winds and rain, Quickfast knew Bellweather, the criminal cow with the enchanted, storm-generating cowbell, was somewhere in the area. What Quickfast didn't know is what the Barnstormers were up to, acting out separately this way.

"Whoah," said Quickfast out loud. "What the heck was that?" As far as she knew, Bellweather didn't have any lightning powers...and she'd just dealt with Lightning Rod. In a flash, though, Quickfast discovered the cause of the sound.

"Holy smokes," thought Quickfast, as she saw these two battling it out, the wind and rain pounding down. As much as Quickfast thought herself something special, a zooperhero like Barbearian was next-level powerful, wielding a magical spear that fired force blasts and supercharged lightning, and summoned frigid arctic winds. Barbearian was almost like all of the Barnstormers in one...but on the side of good.

And yet, Bellweather was going toe-to-toe with her. Bellweather's uncanny cowbell was...absorbing Barbearian's blasts! This, in turn, made the surrounding storm more powerful and dangerous.

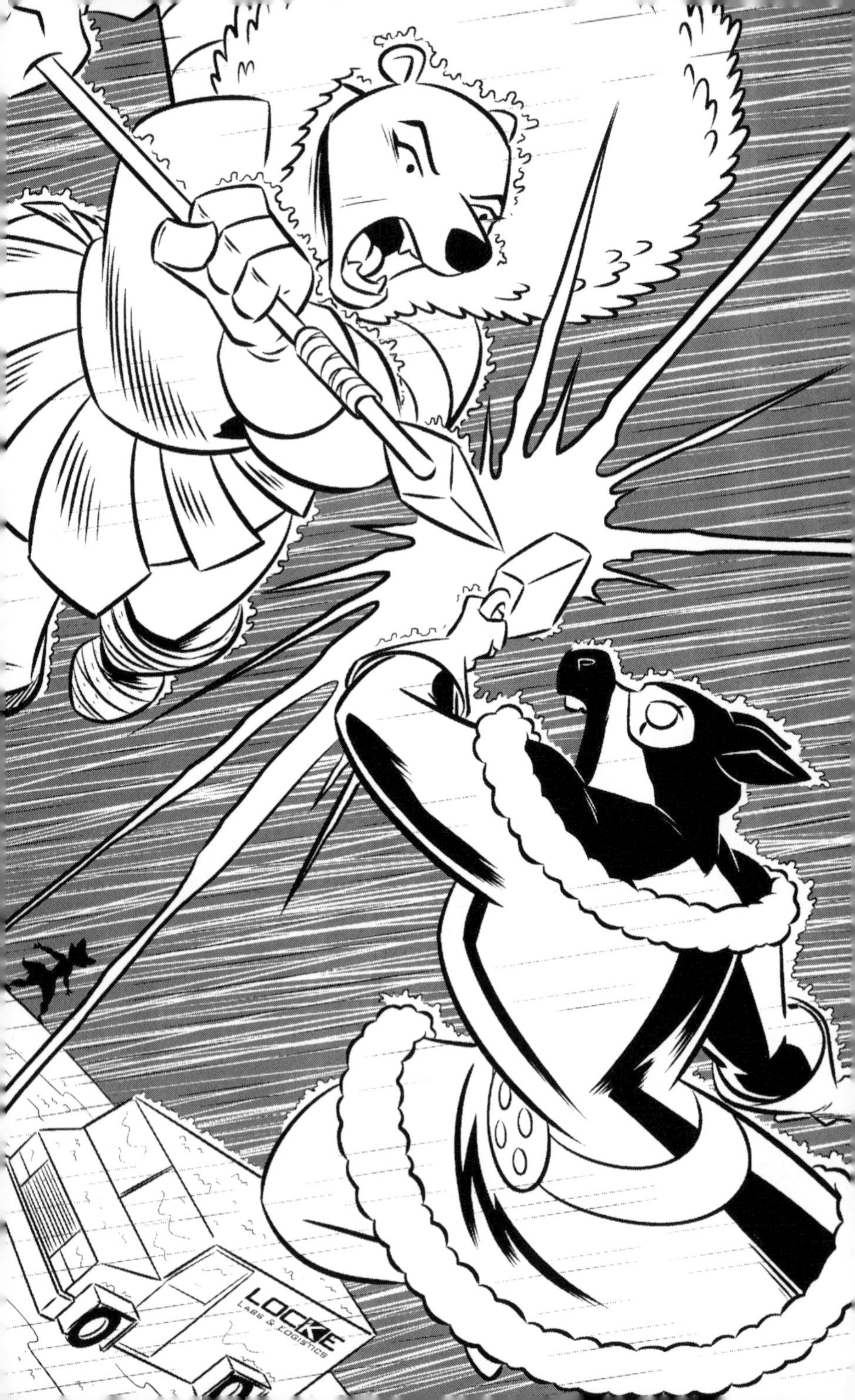
LOCKE
LABS & LOGISTICS

With this situation, Quickfast wasn't sure how she and her speed powers could be of much help. And then things got even more intense.

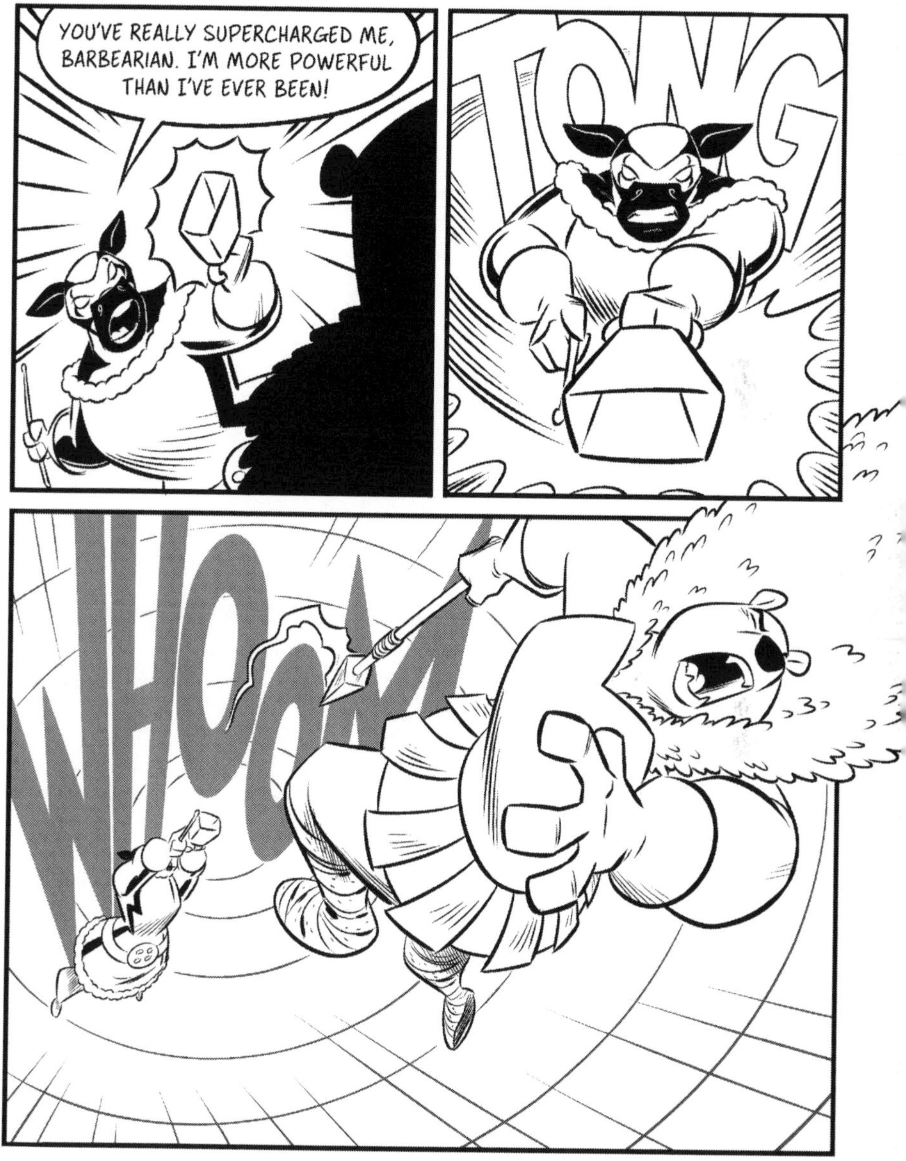
YOU'VE REALLY SUPERCHARGED ME, BARBEARIAN. I'M MORE POWERFUL THAN I'VE EVER BEEN!
TONG
WHOOM

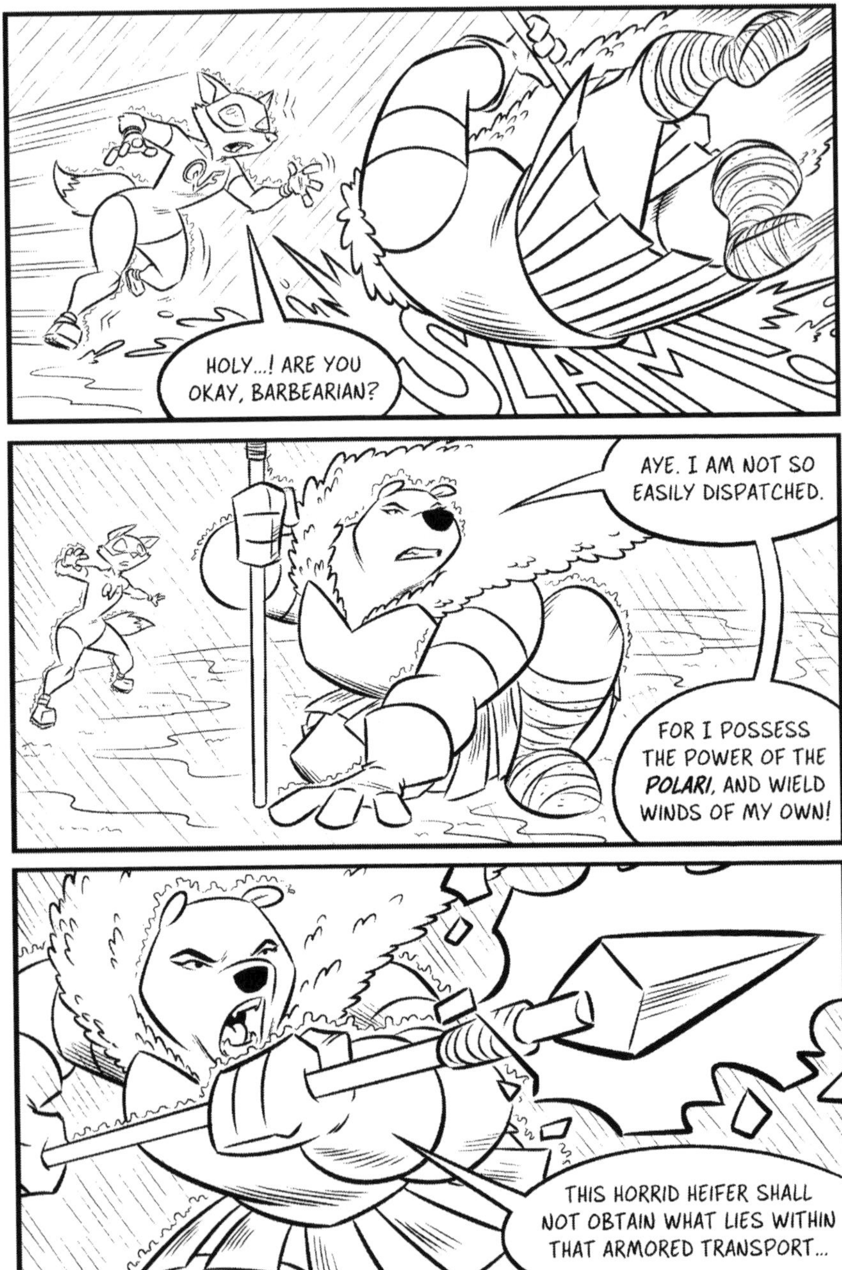
HOLY...! ARE YOU OKAY, BARBEARIAN?
SLAM!
AYE. I AM NOT SO EASILY DISPATCHED.
FOR I POSSESS THE POWER OF THE *POLARI*, AND WIELD WINDS OF MY OWN!
THIS HORRID HEIFER SHALL NOT OBTAIN WHAT LIES WITHIN THAT ARMORED TRANSPORT...

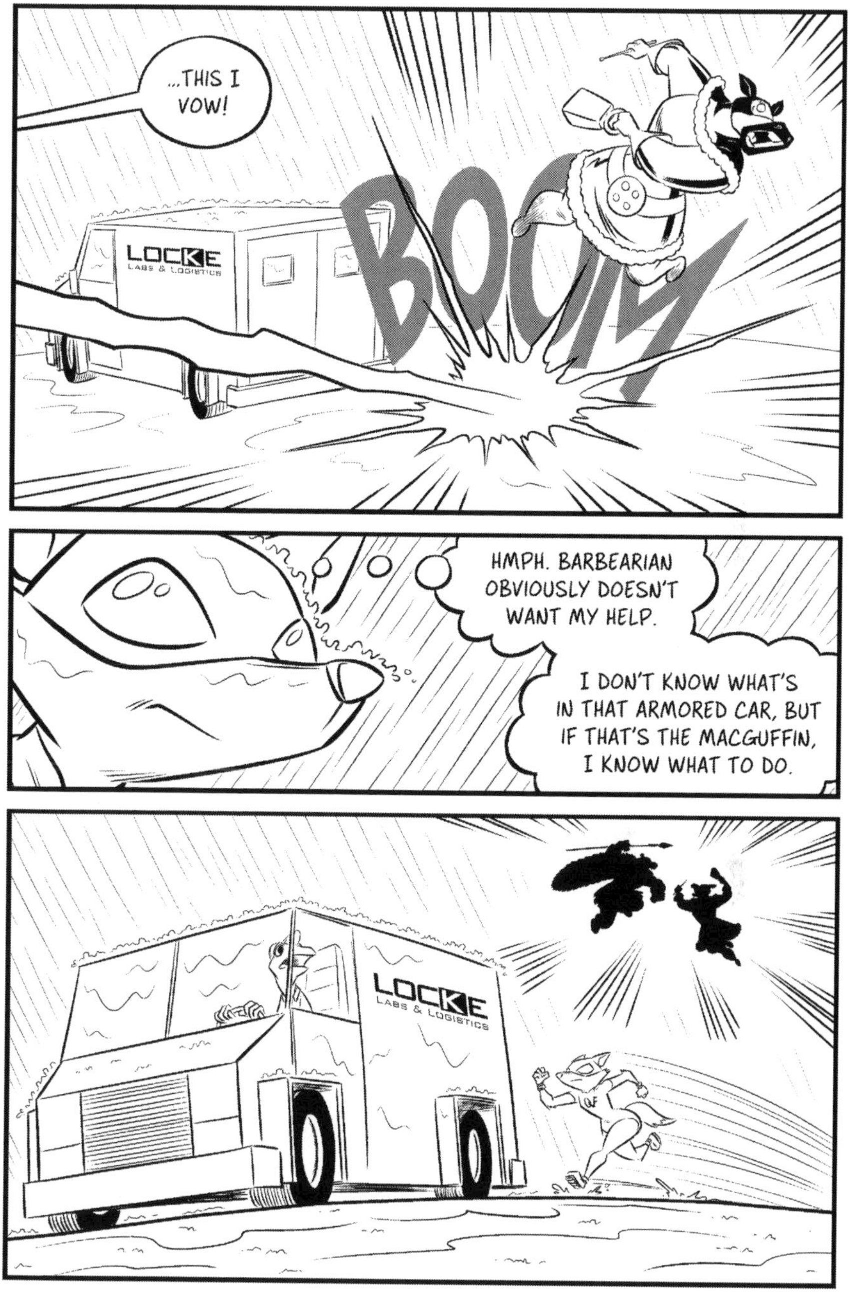
...THIS I VOW!
BOOM
LOCKE LABS & LOGISTICS
HMPH. BARBEARIAN OBVIOUSLY DOESN'T WANT MY HELP.
I DON'T KNOW WHAT'S IN THAT ARMORED CAR, BUT IF THAT'S THE MACGUFFIN, I KNOW WHAT TO DO.
LOCKE LABS & LOGISTICS

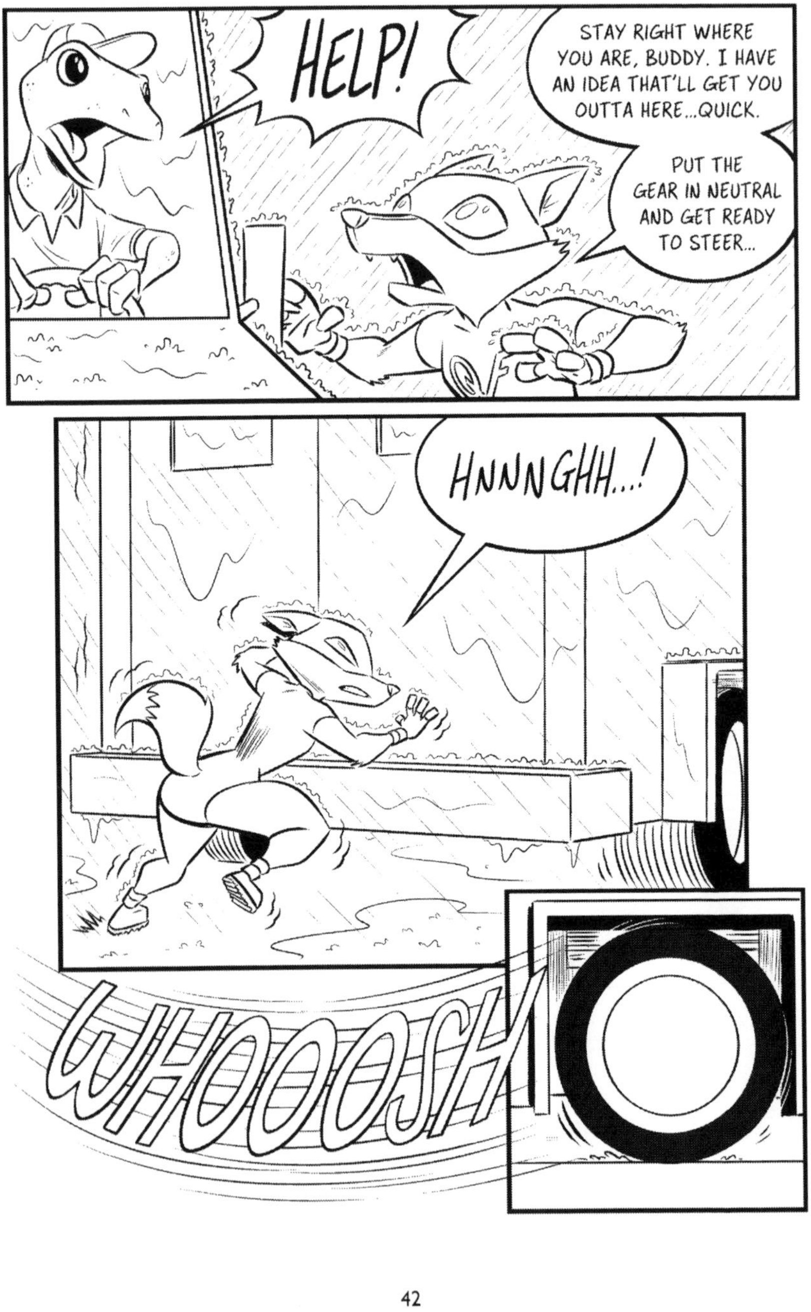
HELP!
STAY RIGHT WHERE YOU ARE, BUDDY. I HAVE AN IDEA THAT'LL GET YOU OUTTA HERE...QUICK.
PUT THE GEAR IN NEUTRAL AND GET READY TO STEER...
HNNNGHH...!
WHOOOSH

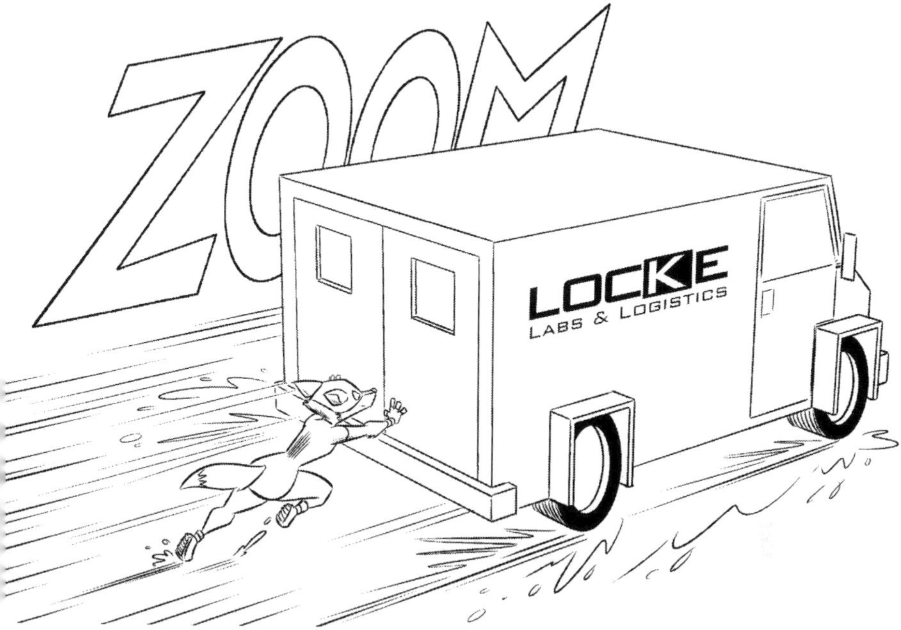
ZOOM
LOCKE
LABS & LOGISTICS

Once they'd reached a safe distance, Quickfast let go of the truck and ran up alongside the driver.

"You okay in there, pal?" she asked.

"Whuh? Uh…yeah?" the driver said, gripping the steering wheel with all his might, his eyes wide. He was clearly still in shock over everything he'd just experienced.

"Well, you're safe now. Put that thing in drive and you're good to go," she said. And with that…

FWOOSH

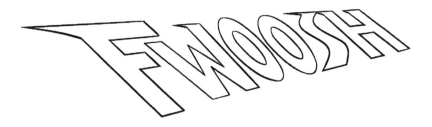

...Quickfast continued her run north toward Delta City.

LOCKE
LABS & LOGISTICS

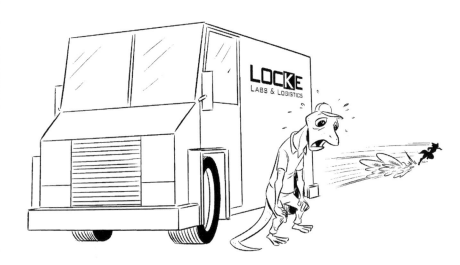

CHAPTER FIVE

Twist and Stretch

As Quickfast ran and passed through Gamma City, she did some math in her head. There were five total members of the Barnstormers, which meant two were still out there, somewhere. She wondered if she'd come across them. Based on events so far, it seemed likely she'd be tussling with them.

Though that last encounter wasn't much to sing about by Quickfast's measure. She wondered if Barbearian even realized that Quickfast had taken care of the armored car. The way Barbearian acted, Quickfast might as well not even have been there. Though, if anyone were to ask Quickfast, she'd explain that she *basically* had saved the day, with *no* help from Barbearian.

Before Quickfast could get too wound up over her bruised ego, she saw a funnel cloud in the distance.

Looked like Twister was the next up. Quickfast ran toward the tornado.

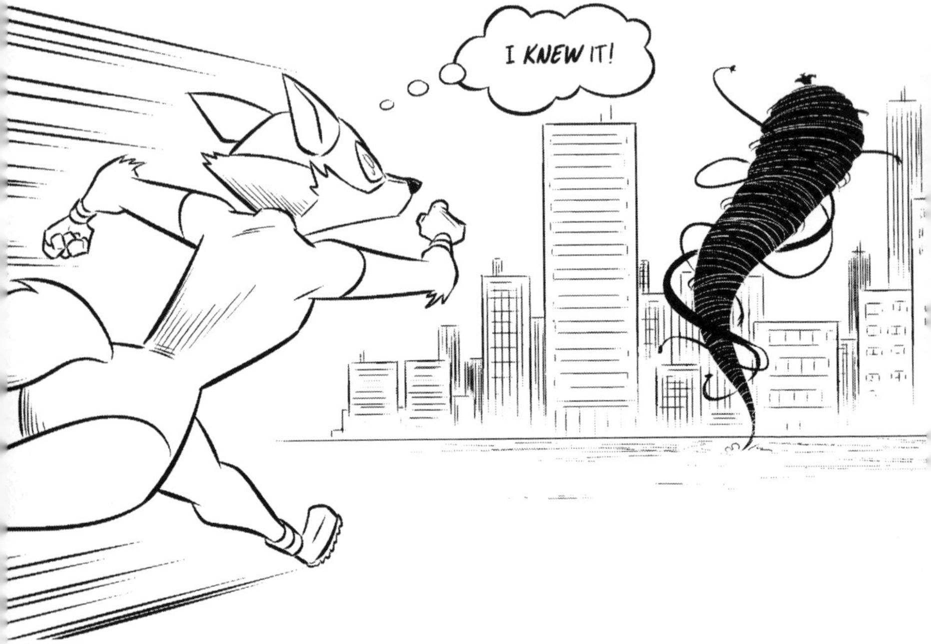
I KNEW IT!

She arrived to discover Twister, the cyclone-starting swine, in battle with Flexi-Bill, the rubber duck. Except Flexi-Bill was severely contorted and out of control.

“Hey, Quickfast! Great to see ya,” said Flexi-Bill, sounding much more lighthearted than the situation seemed to call for. “I’m a little tied up right now, natch…but we can’t let Twister escape with that capsule!”

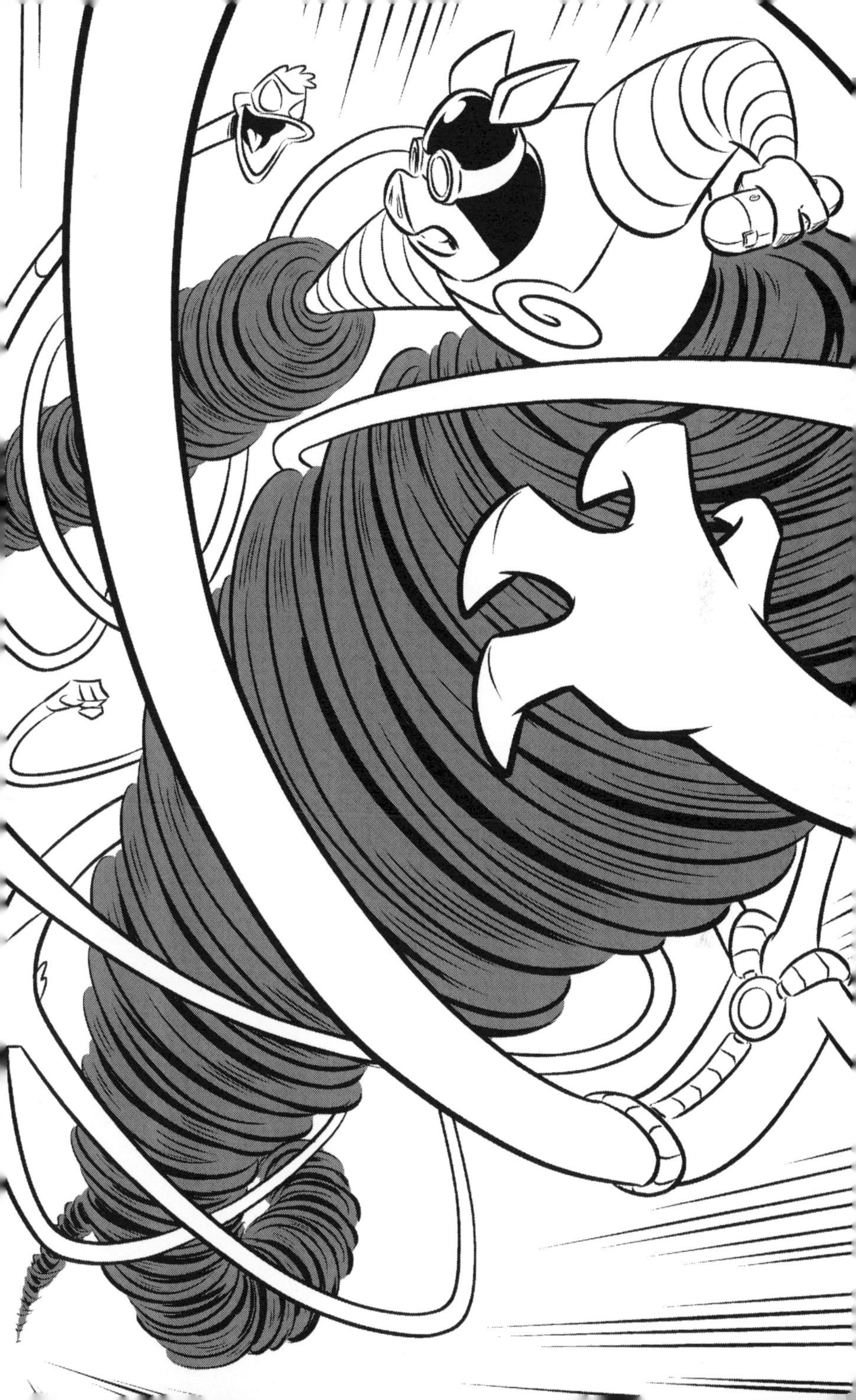

Quickfast noticed Twister carried a small capsule in his non-tornado-creating hand.

"What's in it?" asked Quickfast. She'd had enough with stopping things from happening without knowing what she was actually stopping.

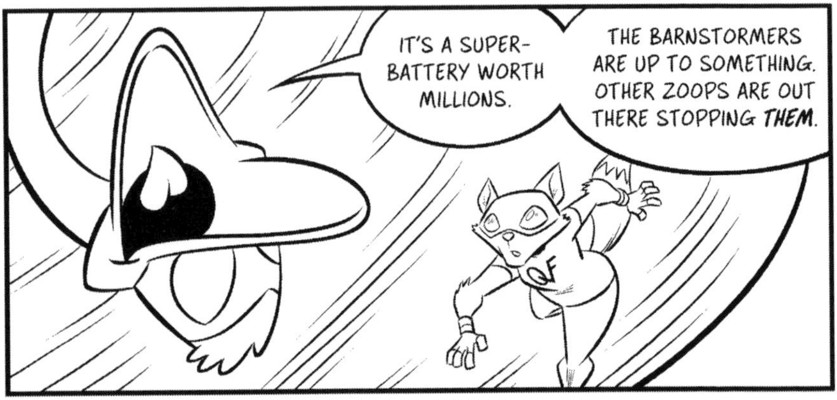
IT'S A SUPER-BATTERY WORTH MILLIONS.
THE BARNSTORMERS ARE UP TO SOMETHING. OTHER ZOOPS ARE OUT THERE STOPPING *THEM*.

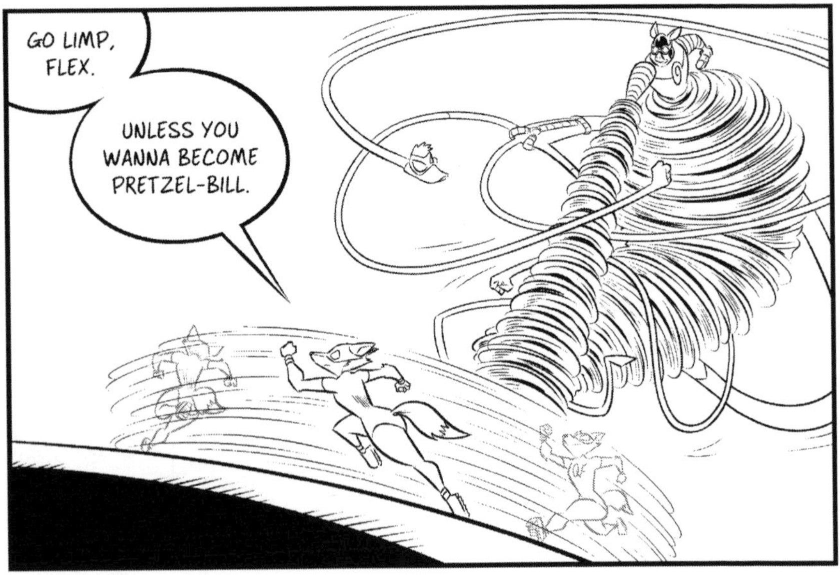
GO LIMP, FLEX.
UNLESS YOU WANNA BECOME PRETZEL-BILL.

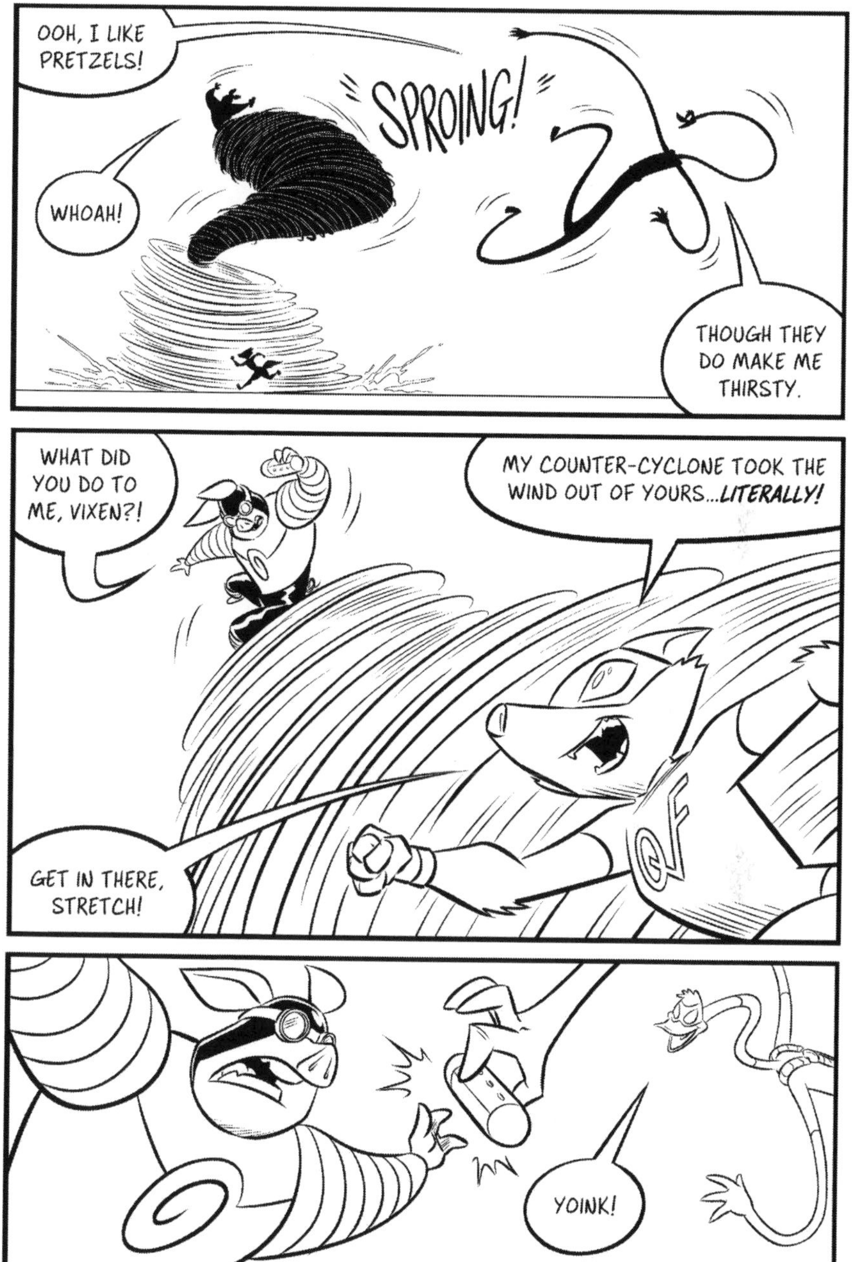
OOH, I LIKE PRETZELS!
SPROING!
WHOAH!
THOUGH THEY DO MAKE ME THIRSTY.
WHAT DID YOU DO TO ME, VIXEN?!
MY COUNTER-CYCLONE TOOK THE WIND OUT OF YOURS...*LITERALLY!*
GET IN THERE, STRETCH!
YOINK!

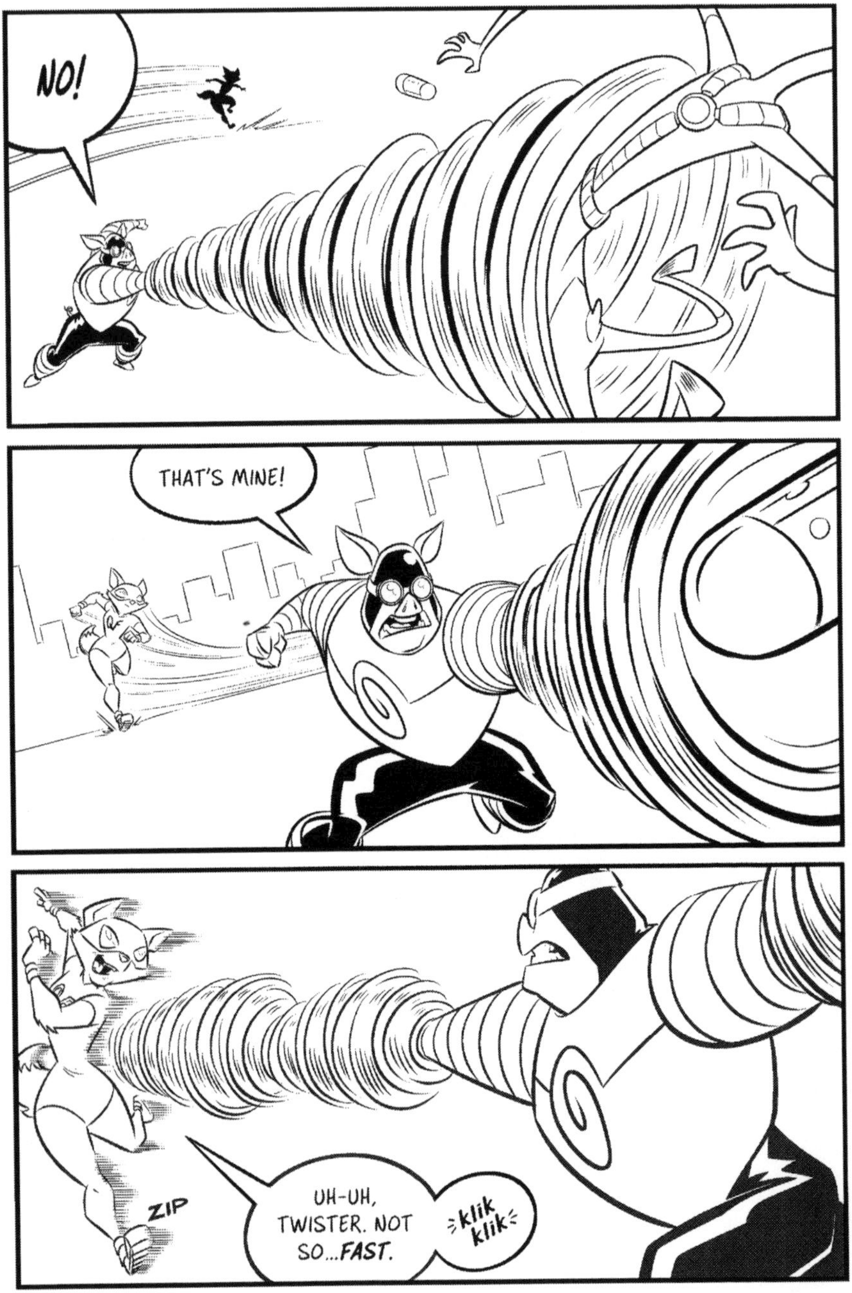
NO!
THAT'S MINE!
ZIP
UH-UH, TWISTER. NOT SO...FAST.
klik klik

WHAP
WHAP
WHAP
WHAP
WHAP
YOU ALL RIGHT, FLEX?
OH, PEACHY...
...I JUST WANNA LIE DOWN.

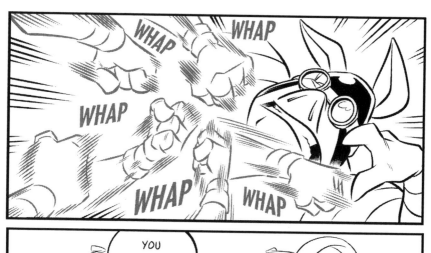

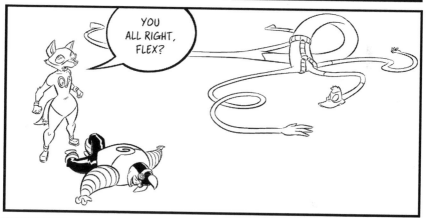

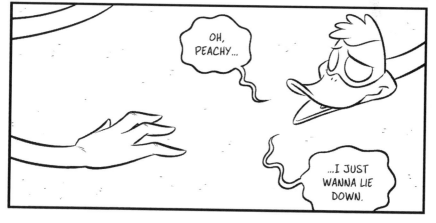

OH, SURE, TAKE A LITTLE NAP. BUT CAN YOU LEND ME A HAND?

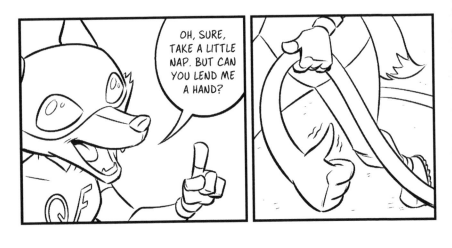

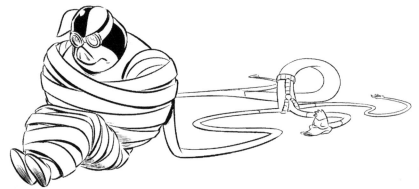

With Twister literally all tied up, Quickfast continued running north toward her hometown of Delta City, thinking, “I’m sure he’ll wake up soon enough and handle things. That leaves one more Barnstormer. Though Flexi-Bill mentioned other zooperheroes were on the case, so maybe I can get back home uninterrupted…”

CHAPTER SIX

Hot and Bold

About forty miles outside of Delta City, with minutes of travel left for Quickfast, the fleet fox was indeed interrupted.

SHOOM SHOOM SHOOM

Hot flash blasts rained down around Quickfast. And while none of them hit her directly, she still felt the waves of heat on her fur. She didn't need to seek out the last of the Barnstormers. Hee-Hot, the high-temperature donkey, had found her.

Hee-Hot was flying behind Quickfast, sending blast after blast of her heatwaves. Quickfast skidded to a stop and turned to face her attacker, zipping this way and that, still avoiding the barrage of blasts.

"You *do* realize I've defeated every one of your barn buddies, right?" asked Quickfast. "So why not just tell me what doohickey you're trying to steal so I can stop you, too."

"Haw, haw," laughed Hee-Hot as she landed on the ground. "I'd heard you thought you were hot stuff. I'll show you heat!"

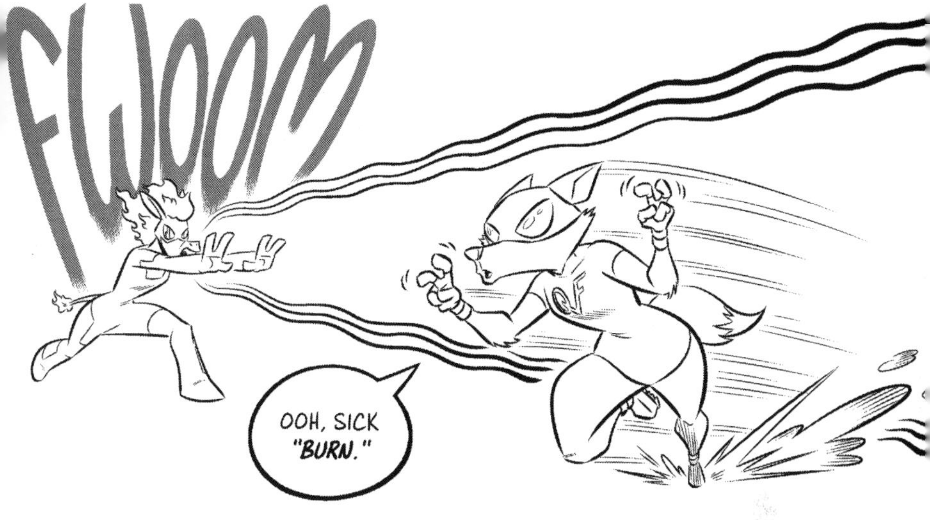
FWOOM
OOH, SICK "BURN."

With Hee-Hot no longer in the air, Quickfast had the chance to make contact. But instead of just throwing punches, she tried a different plan.

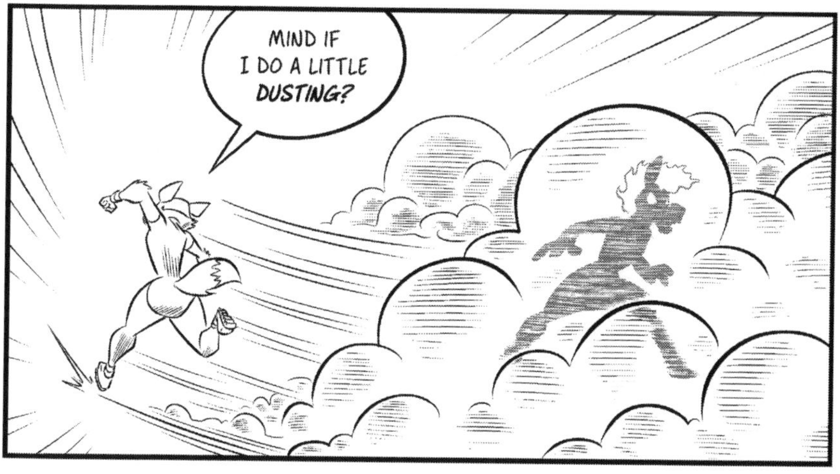
MIND IF I DO A LITTLE DUSTING?

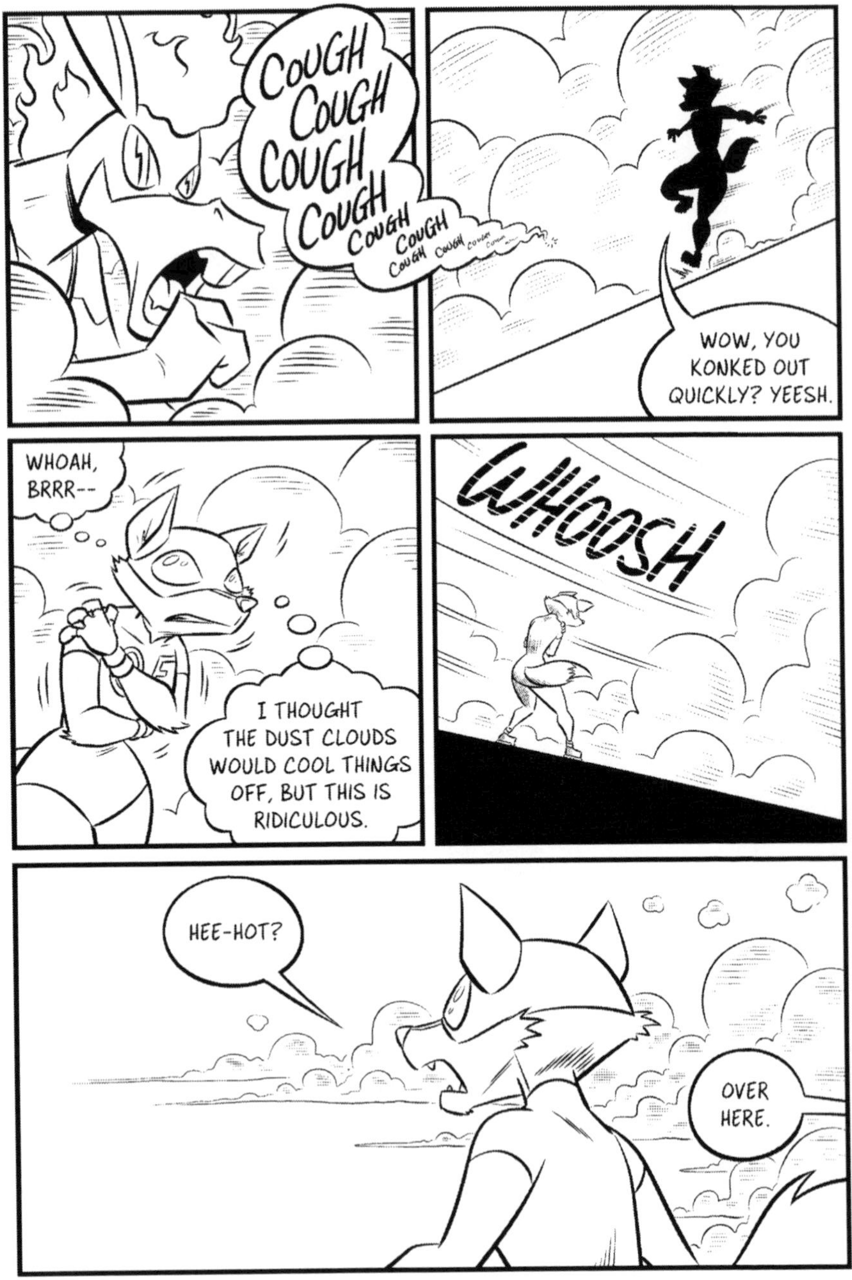
COUGH COUGH COUGH COUGH COUGH COUGH COUGH COUGH
WOW, YOU KONKED OUT QUICKLY? YEESH.
WHOAH, BRRR--
I THOUGHT THE DUST CLOUDS WOULD COOL THINGS OFF, BUT THIS IS RIDICULOUS.
WHOOSH
HEE-HOT?
OVER HERE.

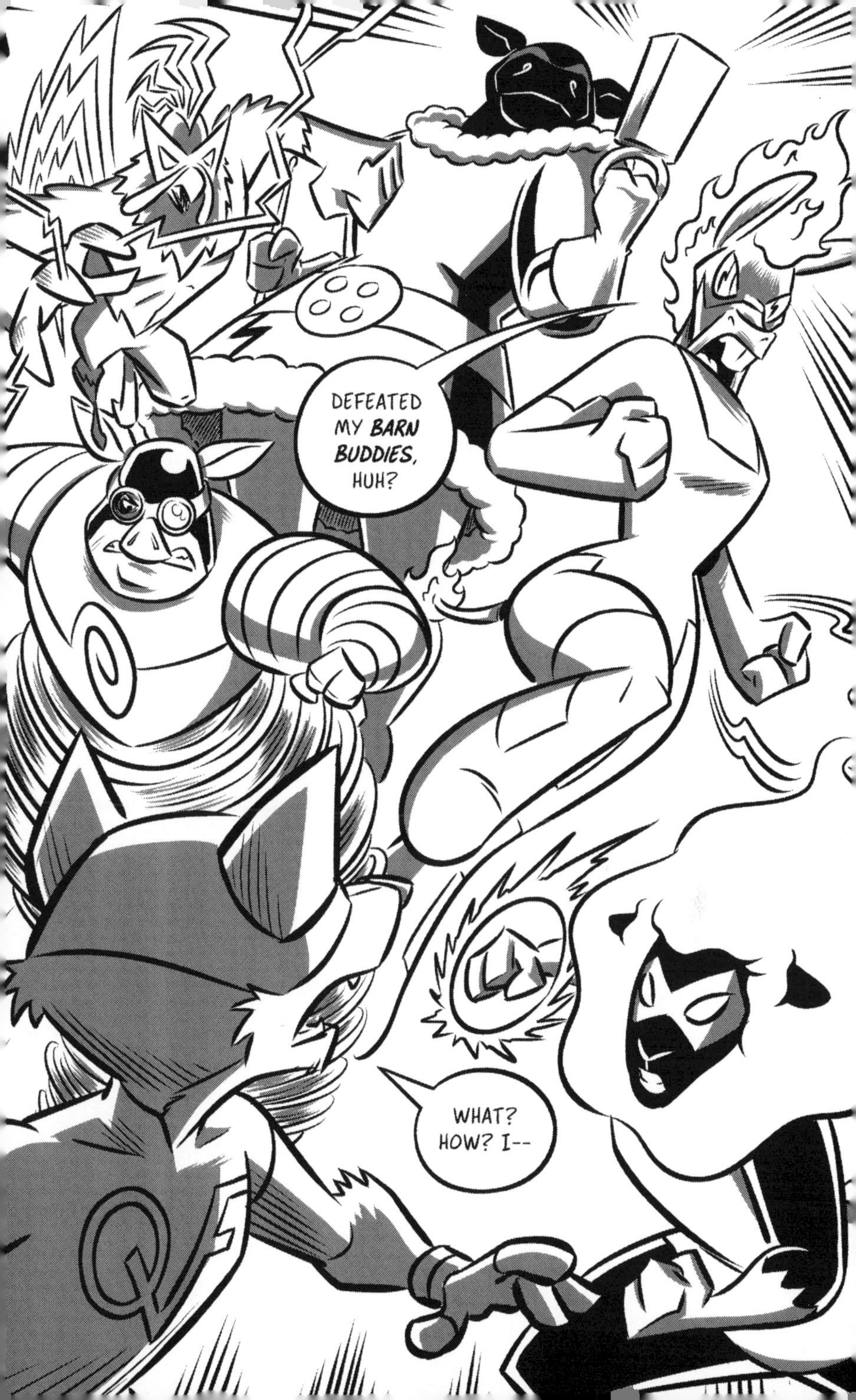
DEFEATED MY **BARN BUDDIES**, HUH?
WHAT? HOW? I--

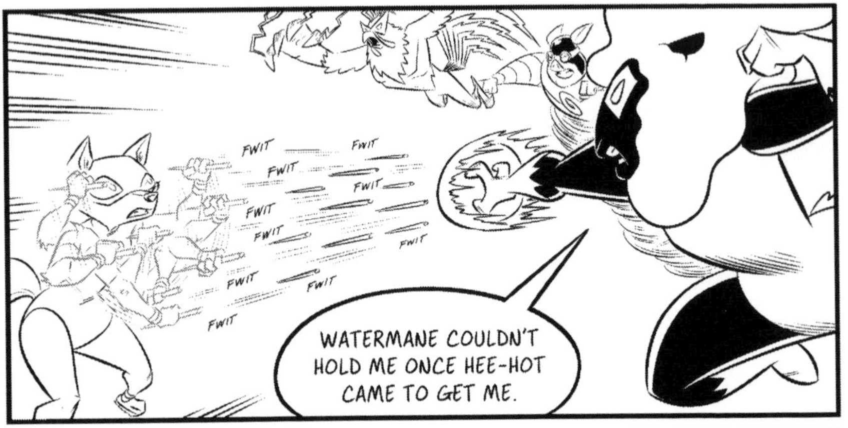
FWIT
FWIT
FWIT
FWIT
FWIT
FWIT
FWIT
FWIT
FWIT
FWIT
WATERMANE COULDN'T HOLD ME ONCE HEE-HOT CAME TO GET ME.

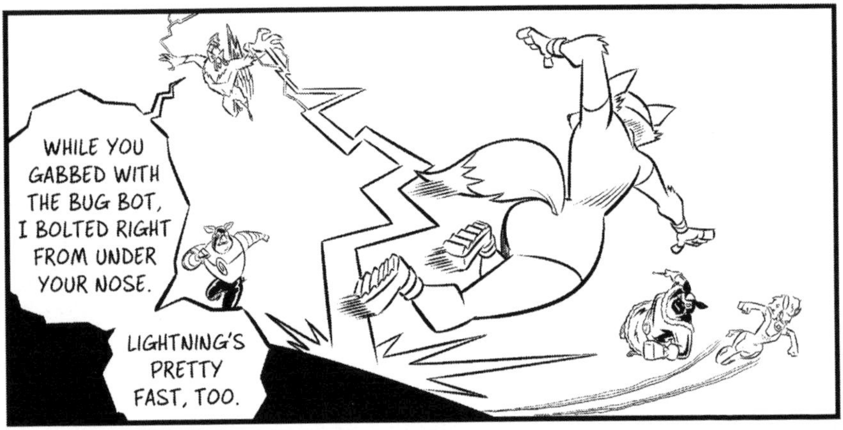
WHILE YOU GABBED WITH THE BUG BOT, I BOLTED RIGHT FROM UNDER YOUR NOSE.
LIGHTNING'S PRETTY FAST, TOO.

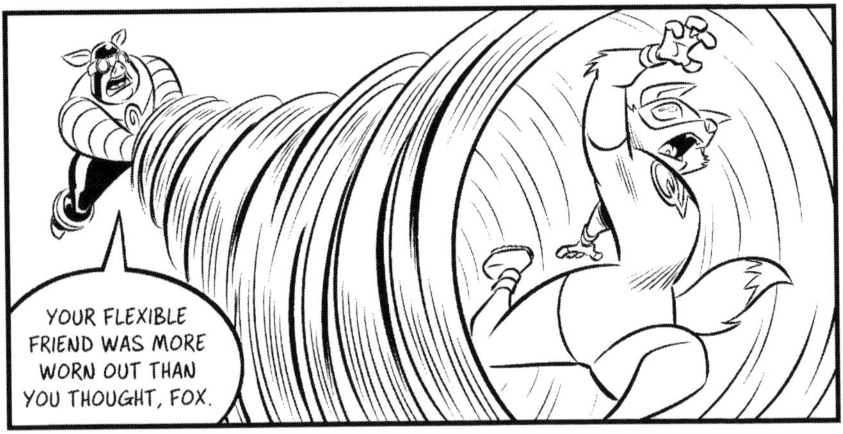
YOUR FLEXIBLE FRIEND WAS MORE WORN OUT THAN YOU THOUGHT, FOX.

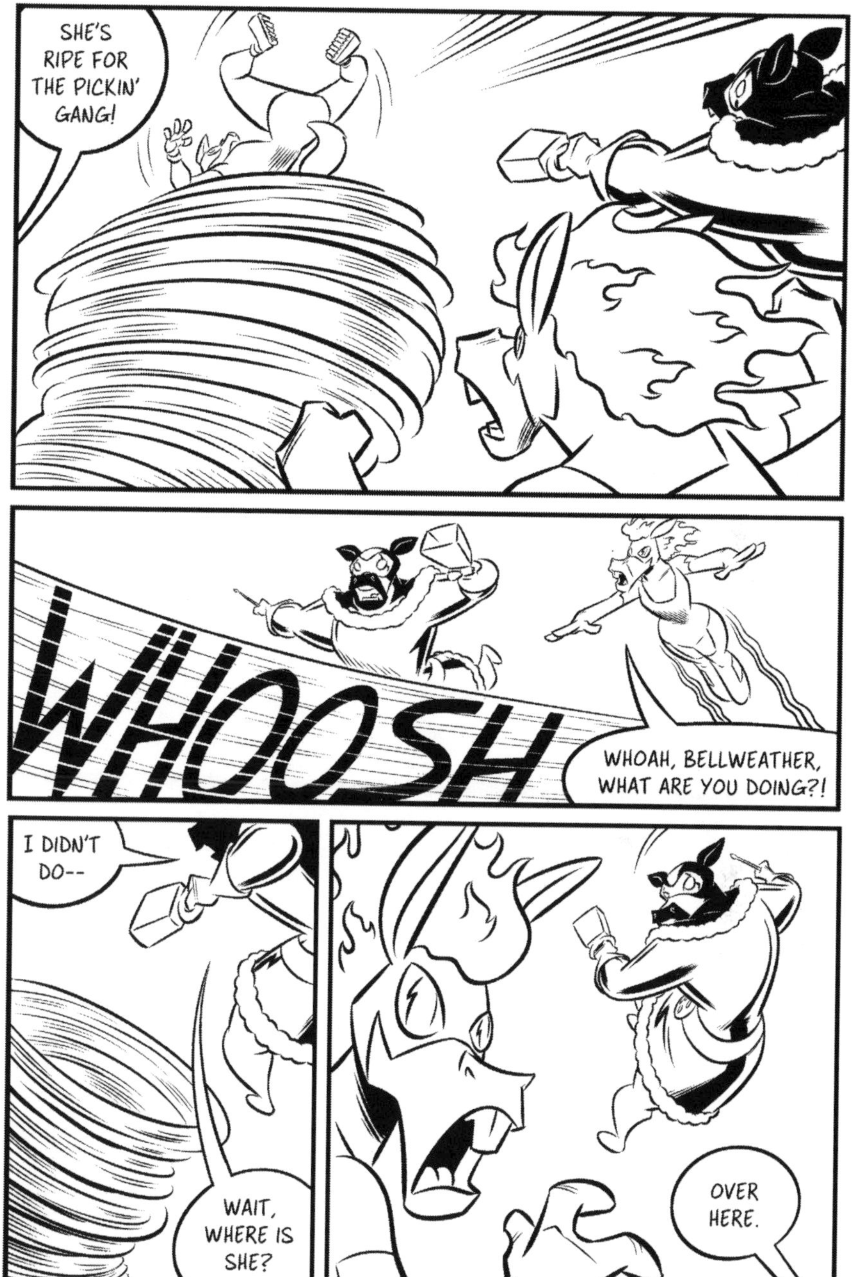
SHE'S RIPE FOR THE PICKIN' GANG!
WHOOSH
WHOAH, BELLWEATHER, WHAT ARE YOU DOING?!
I DIDN'T DO--
WAIT, WHERE IS SHE?
OVER HERE.

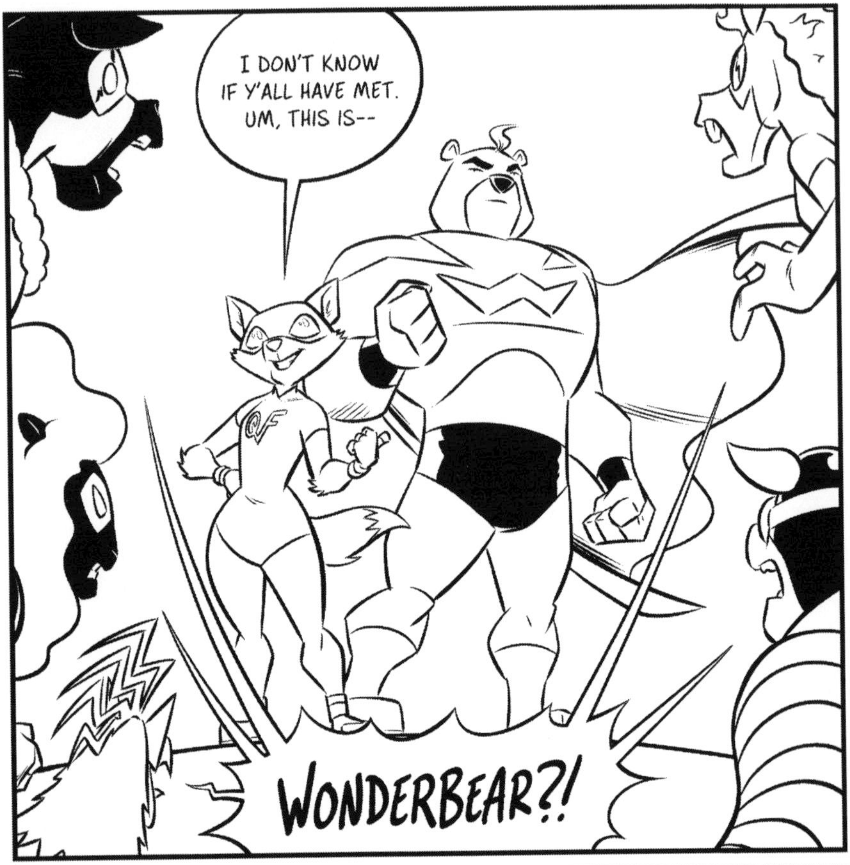
I DON'T KNOW IF Y'ALL HAVE MET. UM, THIS IS--
WONDERBEAR?!

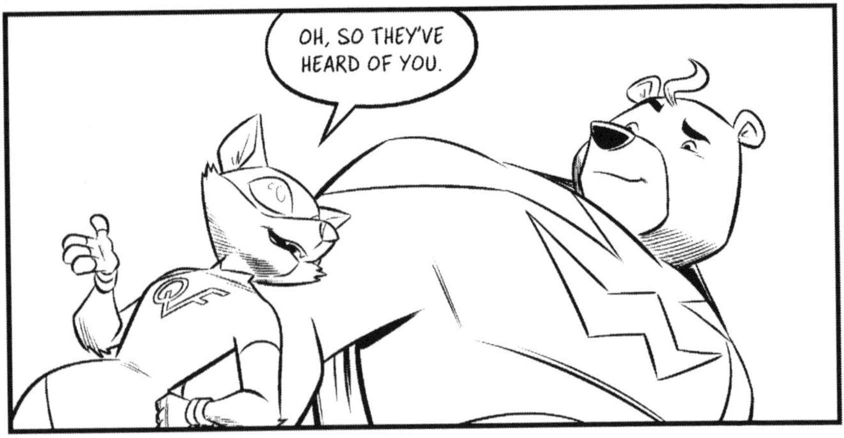
OH, SO THEY'VE HEARD OF YOU.

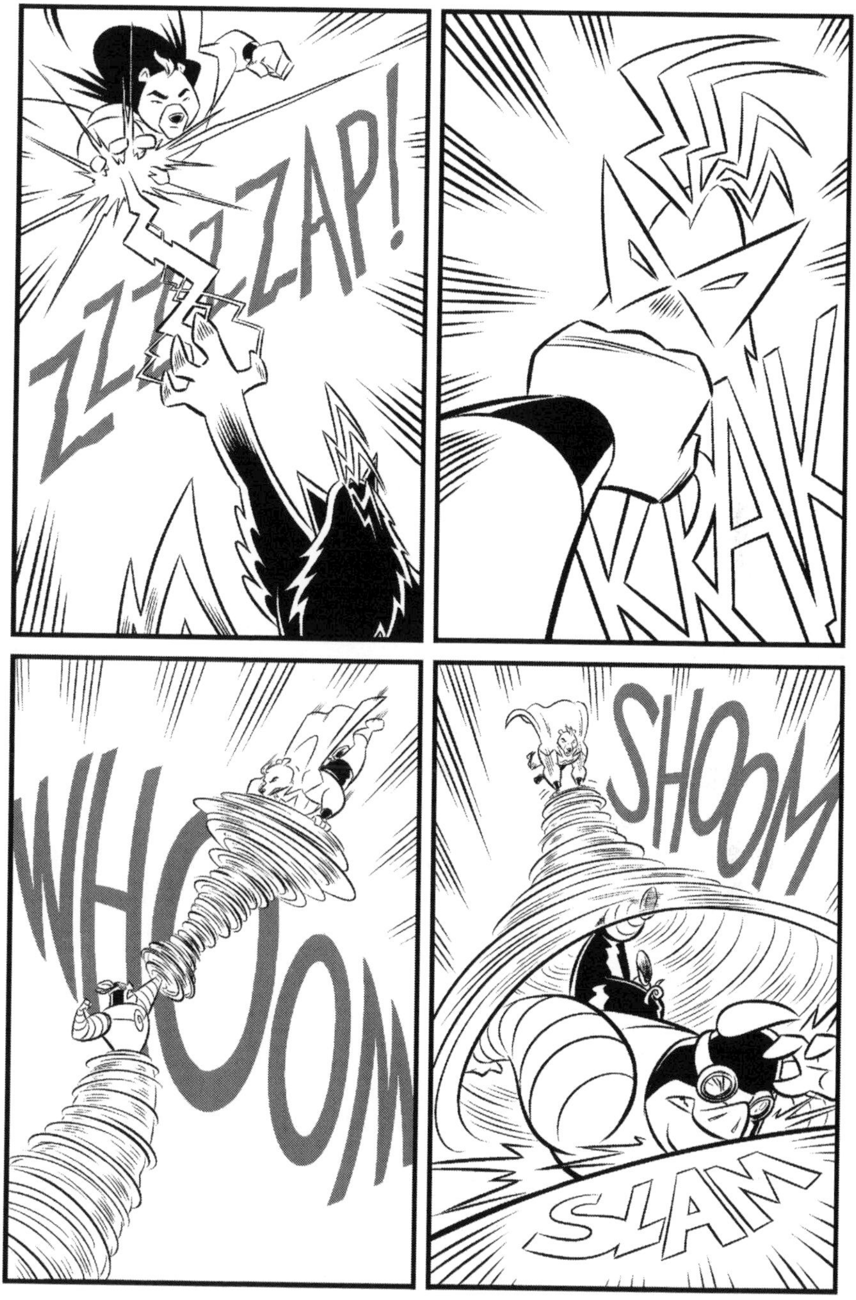

ZZZZZAP!
KRAK
WHOOOM
SHOOOM
SLAM

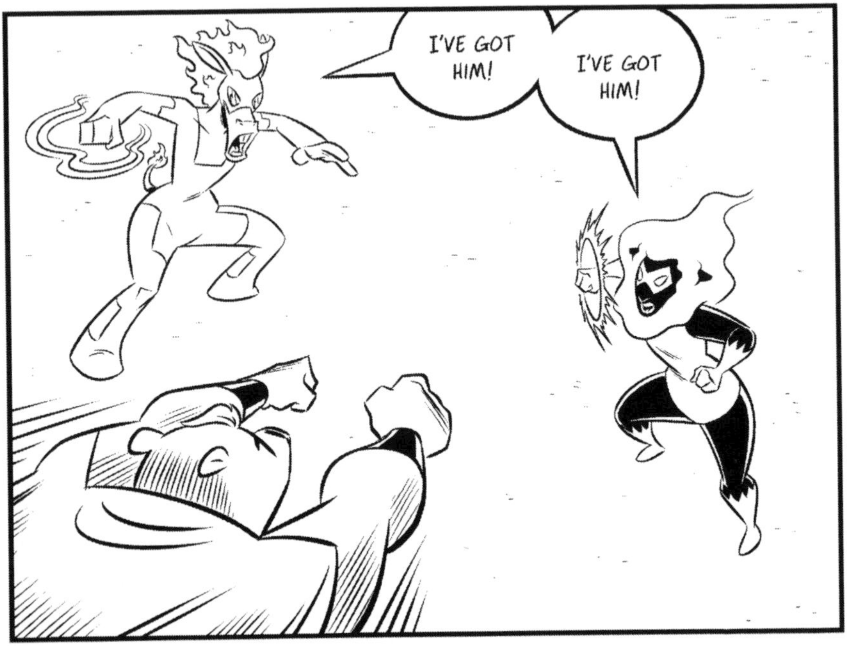
I'VE GOT HIM!
I'VE GOT HIM!

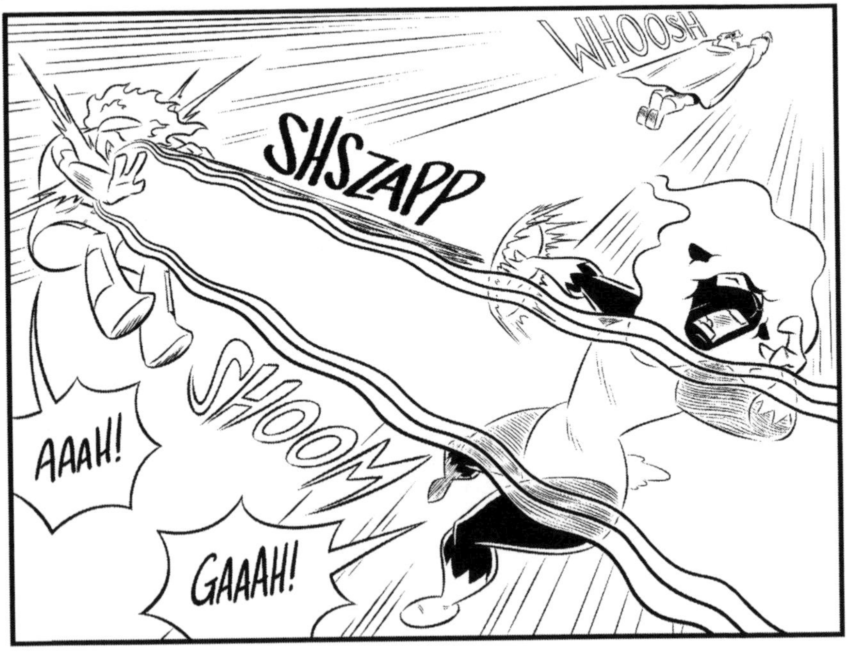
WHOOSH
SHSZAPP
SHOOM
AAAH!
GAAAH!

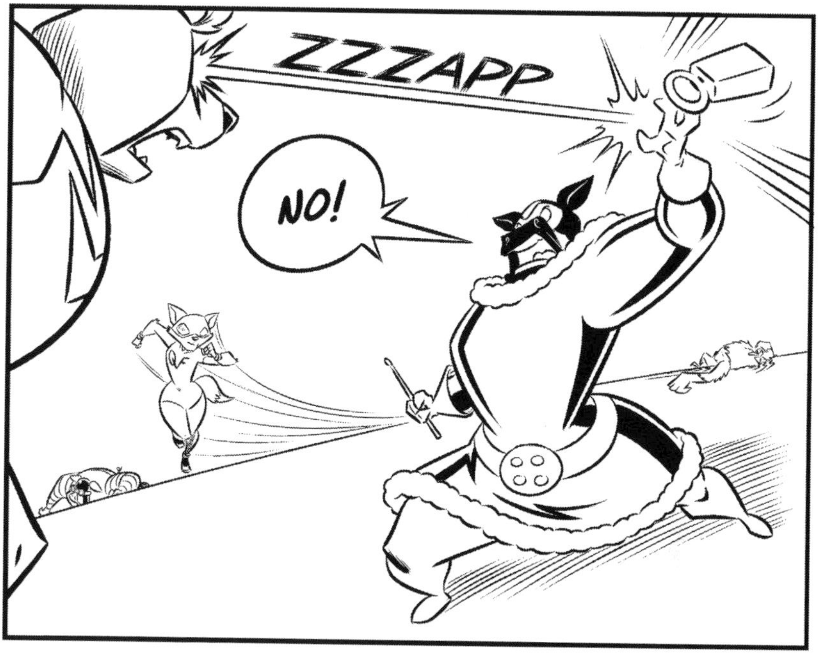
ZZZZAPP
NO!

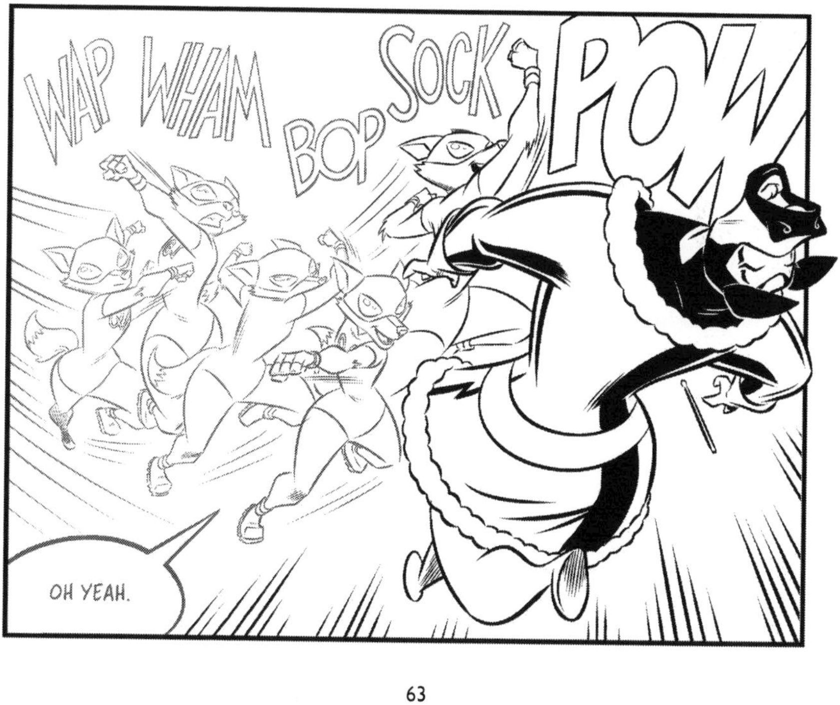
WAP WHAM BOP SOCK
POW
OH YEAH.

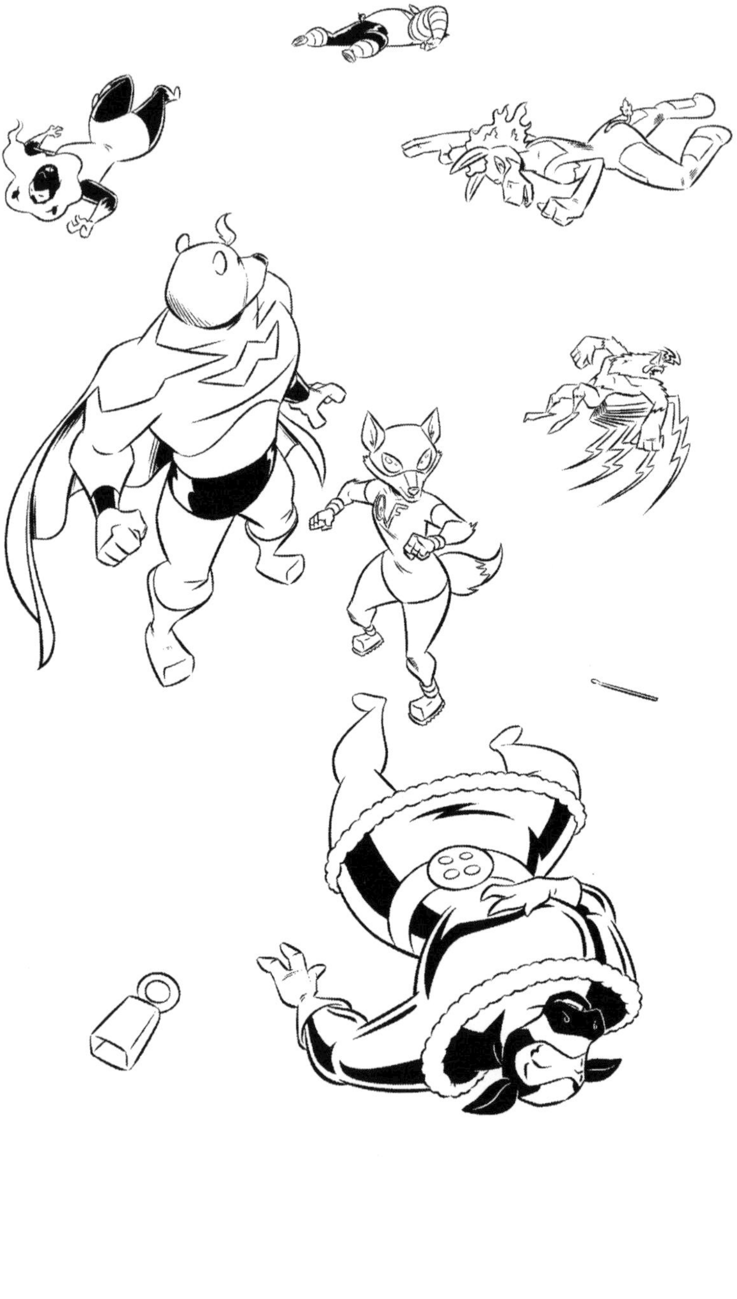

CHAPTER SEVEN

Winners and Racers

"Whelp, thanks for stopping by, big guy," started Quickfast, "That would've taken me—"

"You beat all the other Barnstormers all by yourself, huh?" asked Wonderbear, cutting her off.

"Wait, what?" she replied with surprise.

"Super hearing," said Wonderbear, pointing to his ear.

Quickfast stammered, "Well, that, uh…I—"

Wonderbear put a comforting paw on Quickfast's shoulder. "It's great that you help as a zooperhero. You do a lot of good."

"Why, thankyew," said Quickfast, still very self-satisfied.

"But we do more good together. It's one thing to be a hero, but you don't have to be the only hero. You left a lot of your fellow heroes in the dust before the job was done," continued Wonderbear.

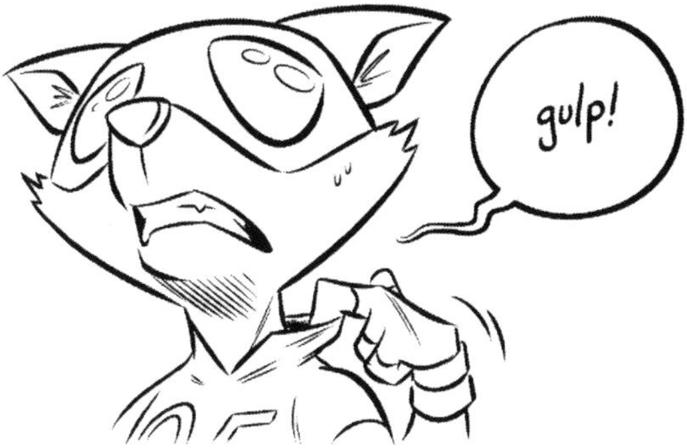
gulp!

Quickfast's attitude suddenly changed. She realized she was getting a talking-to.

"It's okay to get—or, maybe more importantly, to ask for—help."

Quickfast was quiet. She thought about the day, how she'd acted with her fellow zooperheroes…how she'd made every instance about her. Wonderbear gave her a moment to herself.

It didn't take long to think of something to say that changed the mood. She had a quick wit, too.

"Okay, then, can you help me with something?" she asked.

"What's that?" Wonderbear replied.

"Some kids today asked who'd win in a race between us…"

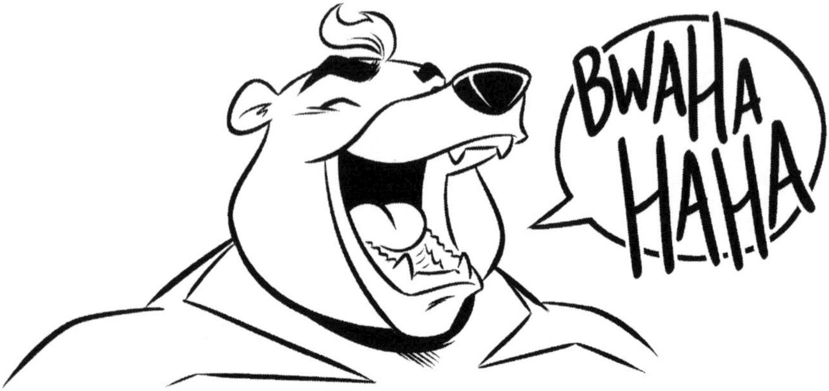
BWAHA HAHA

"All right," said Wonderbear, still chuckling, "we'll have a race. But first, let's get these farm-fed felons taken care of."

•••

With the Barnstormers hauled away by the proper authorities, Quickfast and Wonderbear prepared for their race.

"Okay, so we're going from here to Lake Opal and back, avoiding any large population centers." explained Quickfast.

“Sounds good. I’m ready on your go,” agreed Wonderbear.

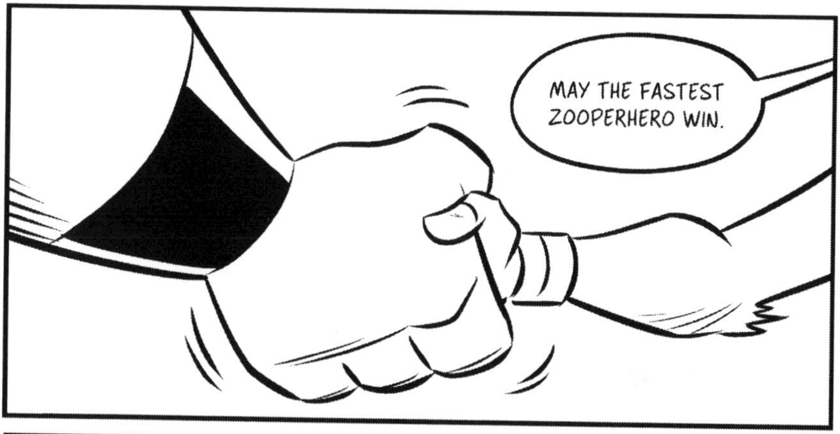
MAY THE FASTEST ZOOPERHERO WIN.

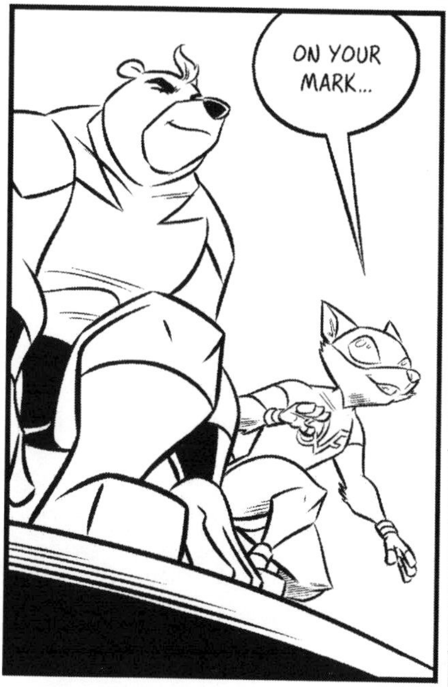
ON YOUR MARK...

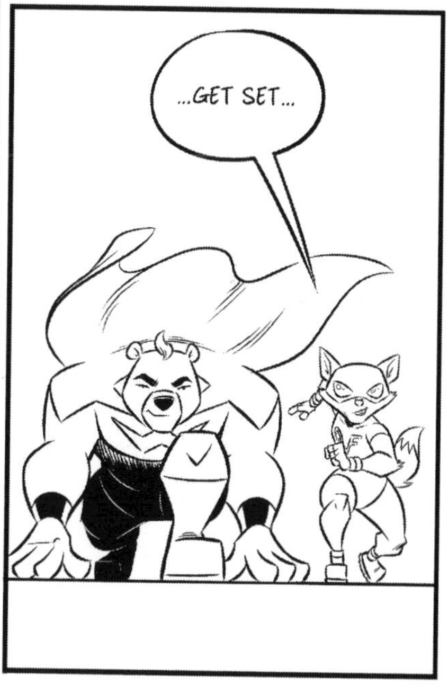
...GET SET...

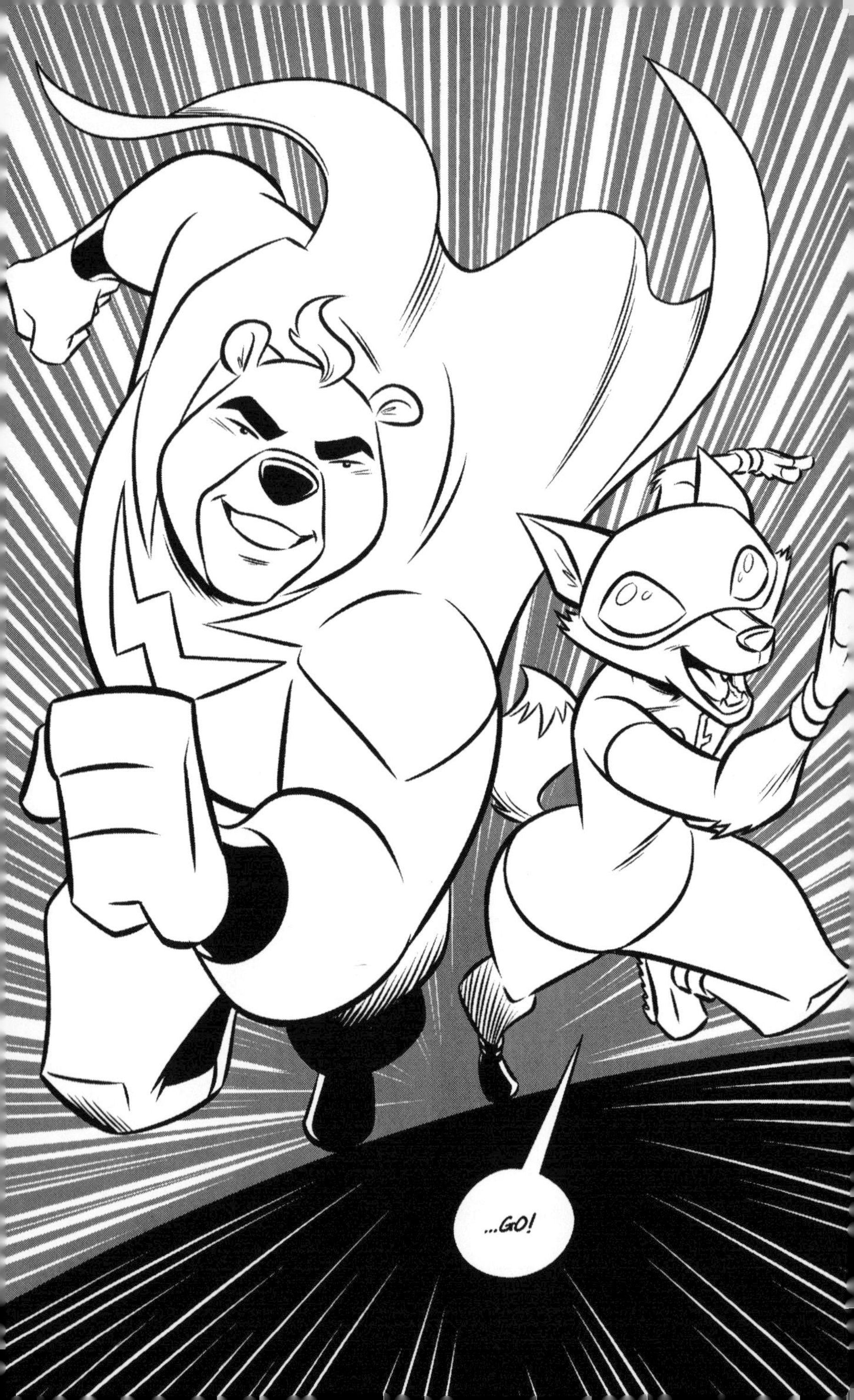
...GO!

They were neck and neck for much of the race to Lake Opal. Each speeding hero had the lead for a few minutes at a time.

Though they made their path one far from any big cities, it wasn't long before news helicopters were circling overhead, reporting on this exciting exhibition.

"Did you tell someone we were racing, Quickfast?" asked Wonderbear.

"Someone had to document it when you lose!" she said, razzing the world's most famous zooperhero.

"You sure do love the spotlight, but we'll see about that," he said, as he surged ahead of Quickfast. This only made her kick into *her* next gear and push ahead of him.

And so they continued, the race still incredibly close. The news copters had trouble keeping up with the turbocharged twosome.

They made their turn at Lake Opal. Still, neither one of them held a lead for more than five minutes.

And then, about halfway back to their starting point,

Wonderbear received an alert signal from the Collared Spaniel in deep space.

"I'm very sorry, Quickfast, but I'm afraid I have to go," said Wonderbear.

"Hm, quitting, huh? Shame on you, Wonderbear," snarked Quickfast, who was several strides ahead of Wonderbear at that moment.

She sped up even more to widen the gap…and to show off a little bit for the cameras.

"Ha ha," laughed Wonderbear. "Well, I'm sorry you won't get your news story, but next time a kid asks, you can tell them you won…"

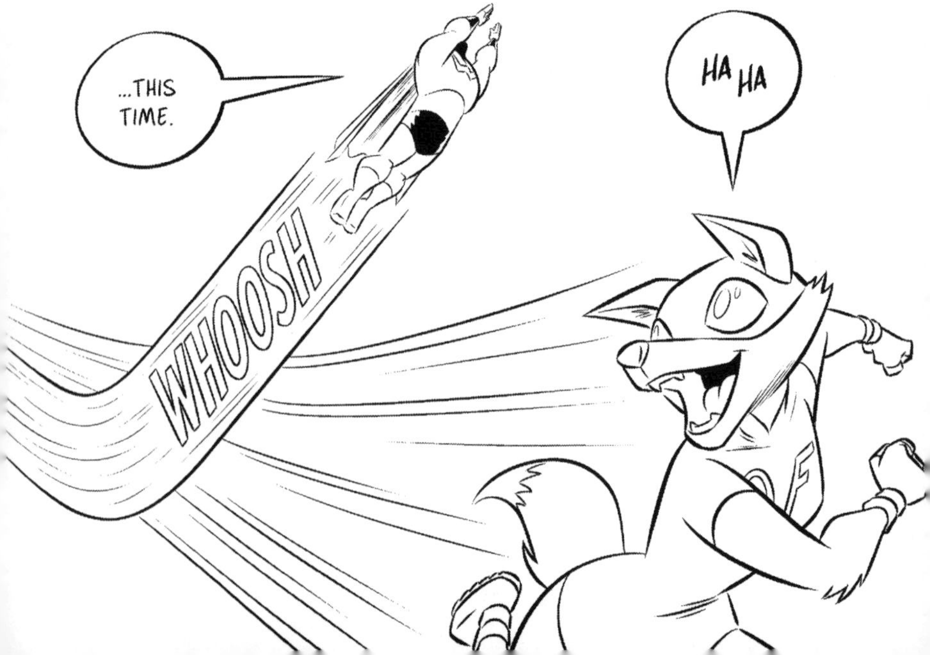
...THIS TIME.
WHOOSH
HA HA

Quickfast laughed and kept running, thinking to herself, "My name is Mika Weir, but everyone knows me as Quickfast. I'm the fastest animal alive."

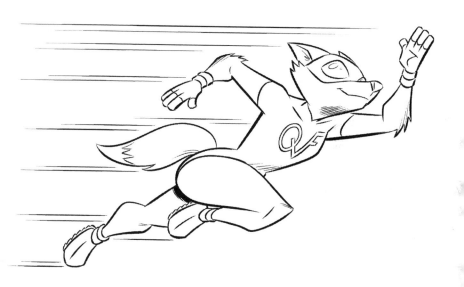

The End.

HERO FILE

QUICKFAST

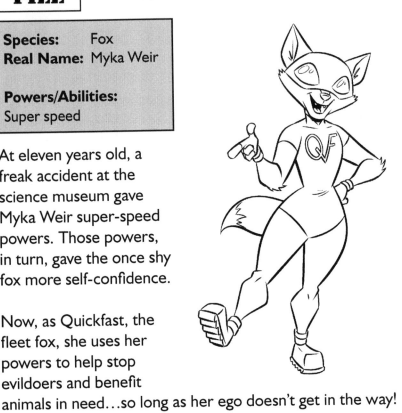

Species: Fox
Real Name: Myka Weir

Powers/Abilities:
Super speed

At eleven years old, a freak accident at the science museum gave Myka Weir super-speed powers. Those powers, in turn, gave the once shy fox more self-confidence.

Now, as Quickfast, the fleet fox, she uses her powers to help stop evildoers and benefit animals in need…so long as her ego doesn't get in the way!

With her incredible speed, Quickfast can run on water and up walls, create whirlwinds, generate heat with her vibrations, and more. And she's not just physically fast. She's a fast thinker and a quick wit, ready with a quip in a flash!

To keep up her energy, though, Quickfast eats…a lot. Her favorite "fuel" is strawberries.

VILLAIN FILES

THE BARNSTORMERS

Species: Varied **Powers/Abilities:** Varied

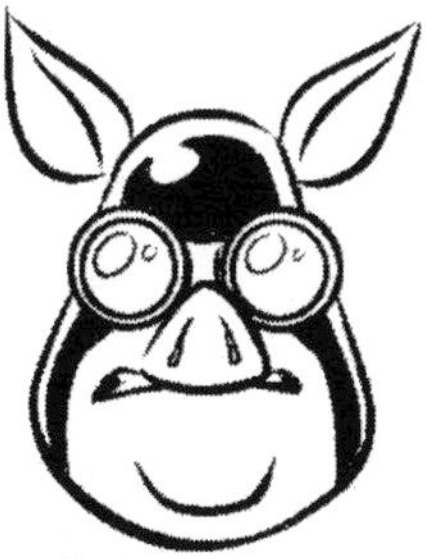

On a secret farm found on no map stands a barn that *looks* like nothing special at all.

But that barn is the base from which the meteorological marauders known as the Barnstormers operate. Tired of their thankless jobs, they've become modern day pirates.

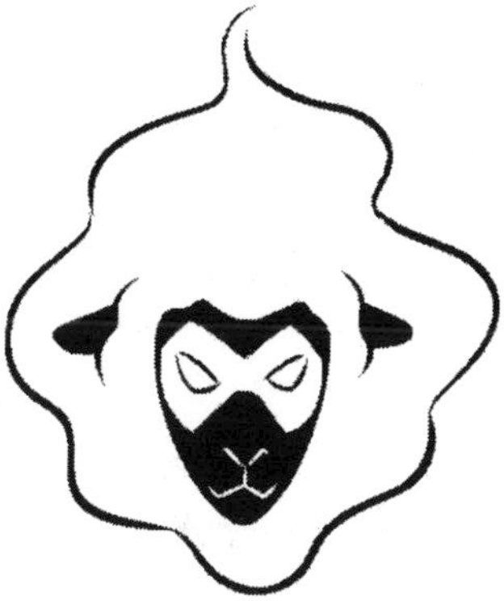

These weather-powered wretches—Bellweather, Coldfront, Hee-Hot, Lightning Rod and Twister—sow their seeds of chaos robbing, pillaging, and reaping the fruits of others' labor.

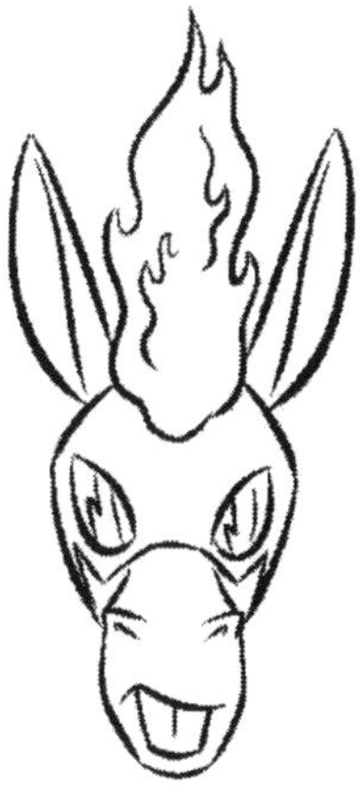

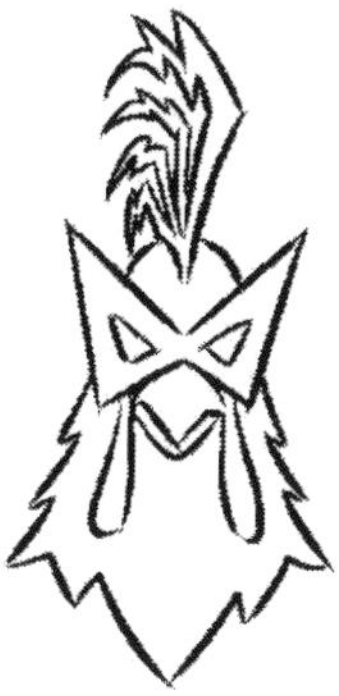

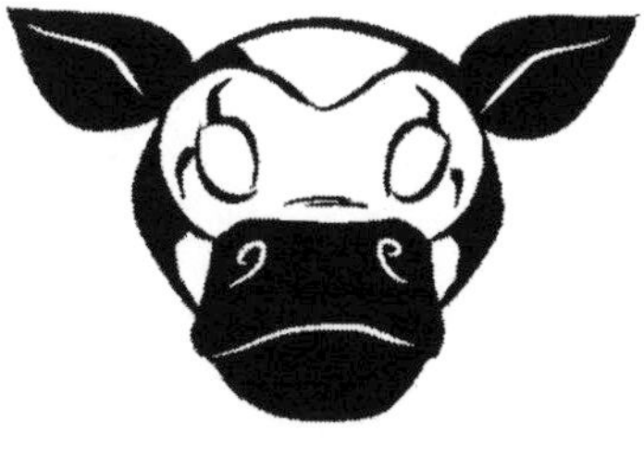

BELLWEATHER

Species: Cow
Real Name: Louise Guster

Powers/Abilities:
Enchanted cowbell controls
wind, rain, and storms; flight

Louise Guster was
a common criminal
when she found and
took ownership of the
enchanted cowbell that
gives her her powers.

With the ability to
control and command
nature itself, creating
rain and wind and savage
storms, she became
Bellweather!

But her power truly
grew when she sought
out and found others like her and formed the Barnstormers.
Now, as the leader of this group of weather-powered pirates
and scoundrels, there's nothing *common* about Bellweather.

COLDFRONT

Species: Sheep
Real Name: Dolly Dewey

Powers/Abilities: Ice and snow powers

Coldfront is ice-cold, in both her power set and her attitude. She's quiet, like a cold winter day, and chilling in the way she uses her powers, firing icicles, freezing opponents in blocks of ice, and more.

HEE-HOT

Species: Donkey
Real Name: Ashley Hale

Powers/Abilities: Heat powers, flight

Hee-Hot has a short fuse and a fiery temper. But even those are outmatched by her heatwave blasts, which turn the temperature up wherever she goes. Hee-Hot brings the heat, literally!

LIGHTNING ROD

Species: Rooster
Real Name: Rodney Reins

Powers/Abilities: Lightning powers, flight

He's the smallest member of the team, but Lightning Rod's true to his rooster nature, always ready to strut his stuff. And that stuff is firing lightning bolts and controlling electricity. Facing Lightning Rod can be a most dangerous wake-up call!

TWISTER

Species: Hog
Real Name: Walter Flood

Powers/Abilities: Tornado powers, flight

Whether he's using tornadoes to fly or shooting cyclone blasts from his hands, Twister is unrelenting when he's on the attack. And while he can be a bit selfish, he's a surprisingly good team player with the other Barnstormers.

MORE ZOOPERHERO UNIVERSE

Available at amazon.com.

ATTACK OF THE PANDROID

NINJAGUAR'S SECRET

ZOOPERHERO UNIVERSE
Coloring Book

ZOOPERHERO
UNIVERSE
ATTACK OF THE PANDROID!
By Gregg Schigiel

ZOOPERHERO
UNIVERSE
NINJAGUAR'S SECRET

ZOOPERHERO
UNIVERSE
COLORING BOOK

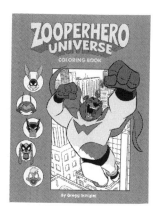

ALSO BY GREGG SCHIGIEL

PiX
ONE WEIRDEST WEEKEND
GREGG SCHIGIEL

PIX
Graphic Novels

Superhero action and fairy-tale magic meet in this fun, funny, and thrilling graphic novel series.

Read free preview chapters and get your copies at **greggschigiel.com/pix.**

PiX
TOO SUPER FOR SCHOOL
GREGG SCHIGIEL

ABOUT THE AUTHOR

Gregg Schigiel (Schigiel rhymes with beagle) fell in love with superheroes, animated cartoons, and comic books at an early age. He loved to draw, create characters, and make up stories.

Now, Gregg is the creator, author and illustrator of the *Kids' Comics Award*–winning PIX graphic novel series and of course, ZOOPERHERO UNIVERSE.

In addition, he's drawn for Marvel Comics, DC Comics, Disney, and Nickelodeon, and wrote and drew many stories for SPONGEBOB COMICS.

Gregg has baked prizewinning cookies, enjoys comedy, and makes sure he drinks plenty of water.

GREGG SCHIGIEL

GreggSchigiel.com